The Indigo Survival Guide

ALSO BY OLENA GILL

Books in Print

The Myths and Truths of Ear Candling
The Question Box

UPCOMING PUBLICATIONS

Books on Indigo/Crystal/Rainbow Children

The Psychic Indigo: A Guide to Spirit Connection
Children of Light series (children's books):
Hello, From an Indigo! ~ Hi, From a Crystal! ~ Love, From a Rainbow!
The Crystal-Rainbow Way

Books on Mind-Body-Spirit

The Twelve "Box" Book series:
The Question Box ~ The Enlightenment Box ~ The Quotation Box
The Meditation Box ~ The Spiritual Prescription Box
The Transformation Box ~ The Affirmation Box
The Abundance Box ~ The Intention Box
The Success Box ~ The List Box
The Manifestation Box

Guidance Cards/Decks

The Twelve "Box" book series

The Indigo Survival Guide

An Inspiring Guide to
Awakening Your True Spiritual Self

Olena M. A. Gill

iUniverse, Inc.
New York Lincoln Shanghai

The Indigo Survival Guide
An Inspiring Guide to Awakening Your True Spiritual Self

Copyright © 2006 by Olena M. A. Gill

iUniverse books may be ordered through booksellers or by contacting:

iUniverse
2021 Pine Lake Road, Suite 100
Lincoln, NE 68512
www.iuniverse.com
1-800-Authors (1-800-288-4677)

Some personal names and identifying characteristics have been changed to protect the people involved in this book and their families.

While the author has made every effort to provide accurate information, such as Internet addresses, at the time of publication, neither the publisher nor the author assumes any responsibility for errors, or for changes that occur after publication.

ISBN-13: 978-0-595-40203-8 (pbk)
ISBN-13: 978-0-595-84579-8 (ebk)
ISBN-10: 0-595-40203-8 (pbk)
ISBN-10: 0-595-84579-7 (ebk)

Printed in the United States of America

This book is dedicated to my loving Crystal child and angel on earth—Katerina—who, from the moment of arriving, inspired me to stay on my purpose. I am humbled and stand in awe of you, and I love you from the depths of my heart.

And to all the Super Sensitive children—Scouts, Indigos, Crystals, Cusps, and more—may your journeys be full of conscious purpose.

The most beautiful sight in the world is a little child going confidently down the road of life after you have shown him the way.

~ Confucius

CONTENTS

PREFACE

Deep down, I believe we all have a natural desire to be understood. I think that is one of the reasons we search for meaningful friendships and for a soul mate, the "one" true person we can be with forever. I believe we seek an understanding to the level that requires no explanation or justification. We tend to connect with people who share experiences similar to ours regardless of how different the situations may appear externally. We have support groups for bringing together people who endure trauma, charitable organizations for people with a common purpose, and political parties for people strongly needing to identify with a community. Such connections allow us to receive a more in-depth understanding of ourselves and the situations around us.

I have written this book for two reasons. First, as the saying goes, "It takes one to know one." It's not enough to talk about Indigos or Crystal children and explain who they are. In fact, that's just the beginning. But *being* Indigo or Crystal is far greater than that, and talking only in a third-person narrative isn't sufficient to do the topic justice.

This book is about being Indigo—what that is all about and how to navigate the way through and be supported in this current system of life. At a time when our global consciousness is rapidly shifting, and old paradigms and belief systems are crumbling, many Indigos—children and adults alike—have challenges coping and "surviving," and they don't necessarily understand why there is so much struggle. It is my hope that this book may help inspire and assist others to know that they are not alone—and that they are not "crazy."

Second, this book was truly guided by spirit, as I believe everything always is. Writing, teaching, and helping others awaken themselves to who they are make up my life purpose.

Although the title of this book is geared to Indigos, for ease of understanding I use the term "Indigo" both specifically and generally. We live in a society that enjoys labeling and categorizing, and our attempts at understanding and making sense of things ties in directly with that. So although I will be describing Indigos as a specific group, I will also cover the next wave of children—Crystal children—and the forerunners of Indigos—the Scouts and Cusps, as well as Adult Indigos. For ease of reference I use the umbrella term "Super Sensitive" to cover them all.

As a Super Sensitive person and now Indigo-Crystal, I share with you the many highlights of my life journey and how I woke up to the knowing of why I was here and what I came to this Earth to do. I share this with all of you who are awakening to your purpose or are wondering if there are others in the world like you. I will unravel the mysteries and shed more light on the individual characteristics of Indigos and Crystals. Parents, caregivers, teachers, and healers will find strategies, coping mechanisms, and solutions for working with Indigos.

I believe that the Indigo and Crystal children in this decade are truly the heralds of a New Age. Helping them and the continual waves of Super Sensitive children that follow to cope and navigate their way around the changing and fluctuating world they have entered willingly is vital.

To your awakening, with peace, love, and joy!

—Olena Gill

ACKNOWLEDGMENTS

There are many to whom I need to express my deepest appreciation for the creation and culmination of this book. This idea has been germinating for quite a few years, and yet it took less than twelve weeks to finally put to paper. This was not an undertaking that I could have done alone.

First, I give thanks to God. If I had not chosen to be here on this Earth at this time, this may never have happened—or at least not in the same way. I am grateful that I co-created this journey with God and awakened to my purpose. This book and many others to follow is a reflection of that.

There are a few people that I must acknowledge: Arnold, Antoinette, Barbara, Caroline, Deborah, Francine, and many more, who have lent their hands, support, guidance, eyes, time, and energy toward the creative ideas and physical fruition of this work. My daughter, Katerina, is especially included. When I wanted to quit more times than I could count, she kept after me to complete the book, so that I could, according to her, start the next one.

INTRODUCTION
The Awakening

It was the year 1986. Fresh off the first year of the university roller coaster with prospects of successful higher institutional learning under my belt, I was a young and restless nineteen-year-old. Although I was unaware of it at the time, the process of awakening my Self was already under way. In fact, it had been under way for nineteen years, give or take a handful of pivotal moments.

By the time I graduated from high school, I was primed and ready for just about anything. And the Universe certainly had plans for me. Funny thing about the Universe, just when you least expect it, or perhaps are ready for it, it delivers to you exactly what you need at exactly the right time.

I was away from home for the first time in my life. It was the summer after my first year of university. I had a job that took up my daytime hours. All of my friends were away for the summer, and I was living in a rental home with strangers. The prospect of going through three months alone, in a strange house, in a strange city was both daunting and depressing. It was as if life for me at that point was colorless—only shades of gray. And then, as if the Universe had planned it all out, Shirley came along—Shirley MacLaine that is, and her book *Out on a Limb*.

I remember finding this book quite by accident. Or rather, it found me. While reading this fascinating autobiographical journey of intuition, psychic development, channeling, numerology, and communication with nonphysical entities such as angels, deceased people, and extraterrestrials, every cell in my body screamed, "That's me, that's me!" It was as if I suddenly woke up and acquired a thirst for more.

And more is what I got. From that point on and for the next three years, all things esoteric crossed my path. Anything that I could get my hands on regarding psychic development, auras, colors, channeling—you name it—I read and absorbed. The more I wanted, the more I got.

I made regular weekly visits to the library to fill my appetite for voracious reading. Suddenly, as I was trying to retrieve a book off a shelf, a stack of them fell, raining on my head. Like Isaac Newton and the apple falling from the tree, *What Color is Your Aura* by Barbara Bowers fell, literally, right into my lap. It was a hard lesson learned in that moment: Be careful what you wish for, because you just might receive it, and be open to how it arrives, even when it's on your head.

Barbara's book was about auras—connecting the colors of a person's energy field with distinct personality traits and behavioral characteristics. Each color represented a type of personality, and her book gave insight to the psychology of human behavior and keys to one's identity and self-understanding. It included a comprehensive questionnaire to determine your own personality color. I took the test and scored high in three colors—Lavender, Crystal, and Indigo.

Perhaps it was the word, perhaps the description of the Indigo personality, but at that moment, my twenty-two years of living suddenly took a different turn. It was like an inner switch was turned on, and I was never the same again. Life as I saw it became a lot more colorful and expansive. Even though the description in her book resonated deep within me, it is only now, in my late thirties, that I fully understand what Barbara was saying at the time.

Who would have thought that it would take a stack of books falling on my head to make me notice that perhaps, just perhaps, I really *was* here for a purpose after all.

JOURNEY OF AN INDIGO
PART I

The Indigo Has Landed

CHAPTER ONE

You are a child of the Universe, no less than the moon and the stars;
you have a right to be here. And whether or not it is clear to you, no
doubt the Universe is unfolding as it should.[1]

—Max Ehrmann,
American poet

It was the Summer of Love. The Beatles had released the Sgt. Pepper's Lonely Hearts Club Band and Aretha Franklin was getting a lot of "Respect." Expo 67 had opened in Montreal, Quebec, Canada, and the "Twiggy" look had heads turning and tongues wagging. There was also simultaneous chaos—race riots throughout the United States, war protesters marching on Washington, and China successfully testing the H-bomb. I prefer to look at it as the summer of evolution, rather than revolution—at least the Beatles thought so.

As I look back, I have to say that I couldn't have been born at a better time. It was indeed a time of evolution, a time of challenges, trials, and achievements.

Many people that I have spoken to over the years have told me that they would rather forget the sixties ever existed and jump right into the eighties, nineties, and beyond. I, on the other hand, find it utterly fascinating. If time travel were possible, and I truly believe that it is, that would be one decade that I would choose to live through and experience.

Amidst all the chaos around the world, specifically on July 10, 1967, I finally decided that enough was enough, that I was ready to experience life on this planet Earth.

Even though I was declared an accidental New Year's conception, and I arrived in the usual way, I was very much in a hurry to get here. I just couldn't wait out the customary nine-month incubation period and instead arrived several months ahead of schedule.

I was already exhibiting the impatience of an Indigo. One look at this life, and I promptly changed my mind. I was told that immediately after my quick and dirty landing, I stopped breathing and flatlined. My existence was touch and go for a few minutes. Neither my parents nor the doctors thought I would survive. After all, I was tiny, underdeveloped, and struggling to live. I managed to hang on and spent my first months on this planet in an incubator. I didn't get to go home. What was worse, I wasn't even given a name until it was certain that I was here to stay.

But deep down in my soul, I don't believe in accidents. I was meant to be here, despite the initial struggle. My inner knowing would prove itself mostly correct, because I opted to stay. But ironically, the theme of survival would last for at least the next thirty years.

Stranger in a Strange Land

Almost every Indigo person I've spoken to—younger Indigos, parents, or adult Indigos—has told me something like: "I never felt that I fit in"; "My daughter tells me that she's different"; "I never felt as if I belonged here."

All have in some fashion expressed an unhappy emotion—discomfort, anger, restlessness, or discontentment at feeling out of place on this Earth. Some even joked with me about being deposited on Earth by aliens, because they didn't feel connected or have a sense of belonging. Moreover, as I will discuss further in this book, they intuit the fact that they feel different, and people around them, though familiar, seem like strangers. And they go through their lives with the deep longing of searching for others like them.

I could relate to all of that. My earliest memories of myself were that I was aware of my own existence, and that I had the feeling of being the "foreigner in one's own country." Both came when I was about four years old. When I got older I would wonder when consciousness and self-awareness actually kicks in. I have absolutely no conscious memory of who I was before four years of age. But even then, I already felt uncomfortable at the recognition that I actually existed. I believe at that point, I had my first conscious sense of my soul—that there was a part of me that was greater than my body. I also became painfully aware of how constricting it felt to be in my body. The trouble was that I didn't know how to deal with it.

The house I grew up in was small. There was not a lot of room, especially with my much older brother needing his own space. At the age of four, I was still sleeping in a crib crammed into my parents' bedroom. Apparently I had a habit of escaping out of bed like Houdini and sleepwalking at night, so someone had to keep an eye on me.

On one bright sunny day I remember waking and looking around the room that I was in. Directly across from my bed, there was an icon of Jesus and Mother Mary.

My family was Ukrainian and very religious. Every icon in our home and in the culture was Byzantine, a form of period art, typical of Eastern European cultures.

To briefly give a quick historical background, Byzantine art was prevalent during the Eastern Roman Empire in the Middle Ages. Mosaic depictions of religious or saintly figures of the Christian tradition were the norm, but in an extremely humanistic way. It is not uncommon to see God, Jesus, and Mother Mary portrayed separately or as a trio in these icons. The purpose of these icons was to allow mankind to see the spiritual essence of the subjects and thus facilitate a closer inner connection.

These realistic icons played a huge role in my life. The icons were practically three-dimensional, and every time I stared at their eyes, it seemed like they were very much alive and staring right through me. I now know that they helped visually connect me to the larger energy of the Universe, becoming conscious of my psychic abilities.

But at four, if I tried hard enough, it was as if I could hear Jesus speaking to me.

There was already a stirring and a knowing inside of me that although I was staring at a painting, the notion of tapping into something greater than me was there. Those icons, especially Jesus, became a source of great comfort in my life as more and more adversity crossed my path in my later years.

As I stood there in my crib, readying myself to make the great escape and looking around the room, there was a part of me that seemed to recognize things that were familiar. I could identify my parents' bed, the dresser, the closet.

But simultaneously, I had the strong feeling that I was in a foreign place, as if I had just arrived from someplace unknown and dropped in. It was familiar, yet strange. I thought it was a dream.

Very quickly, the stark reality hit me, as if someone had poured cold water over my head. It was not a dream. I was here. I was in this body. And I was not going anywhere.

My body felt so constricted, so limited. It was an intense, uncomfortable feeling—a feeling of being trapped and having no control to change the circumstances around me. Right then, I knew that I did not want to be there, and I felt incredibly angry and rebellious for a four-year-old.

Get me out of here, please, I silently screamed to myself as I locked eyes with Jesus. I squeezed my eyes tightly over and over again, willing myself to disappear. Crying by this time, I kept pleading with the face of Jesus—*Take me away, I don't like it here!* And strangely enough, through the tears, I swore I heard words coming from somewhere far away, saying, "Olena, it's all right. I love you."

But I did not disappear. At that moment, when I realized that my inner wish was not granted, it was if a switch shut off inside of me, like a light going out in a room. It was that kind of switch that makes one feel like they are connected to something, but for me, that ended right there. My energy went down. I became unhappy. And that switch didn't turn on again until almost twenty years had passed.

It had been a bumpy ride, but I definitely had landed. Where exactly, was harshly clear. Why, still remained a great mystery. But that of course quickly started revealing itself, in school.

Early Shapings

CHAPTER TWO

There is one thing in this world, which you must never forget to do.
Human beings come into this world to do particular work.
That work is their purpose, and each is specific to the person.
If you forget everything else and not this, there's nothing to worry about.
If you remember everything else and forget your true work,
then you will have done nothing in your life.²

—Rumi
Sufi poet and mystic

As she looked around the room at the restless bunch of five-year-olds, Ms. McDonald asked "So what do you want to be when you grow up?" At least a dozen small arms shot up in the air, waving wildly.

"Me, me, pick me," they yelled, every little voice competing with each other, trying to be heard first.

"Olena, what do you want to do?" Ms. McDonald asked, as she looked at me, smiling.

She knew that I had a tendency to be shy and spoke very little. I also lisped and had a funny accent, because English was not my first language. I avoided speaking as much as possible and preferred to let the noise of the other excited children wash right over me. But as an astute teacher, it was no surprise that she honed right in on me.

"Well," I said, trying to sound thoughtful for a five-year-old kid, "I like to read books, and I like to type on the typewriter!" I silently hoped this would soon be over.

"Maybe you can grow up to be a writer someday," Ms. McDonald said. I let those words wash right over me.

Writer? I didn't even know what a writer really did! The truth was that I did not know what I wanted to do. Most five year old children don't. I had no concept of what the rest of my life would be, much less trying to picture what I would look like grown up. But strangely enough those words rang a bell somewhere deep inside of me and that feeling stayed with me throughout my formative years. They touched something familiar, yet I was unaware of what that was yet.

My interest was piqued. I decided to pursue this further. "Ms. McDonald," I said, "did you want to be a teacher when you grew up?"

"No, Olena. In fact let me tell you my story about what I wanted to do as a little girl," she said. "I used to skate as a little girl. I skated all the time, and I dreamed of being a championship skater. All I wanted to do was skate, skate, and skate. Nothing else."

I listened with great rapture. "So what happened, Ms. McDonald?" I asked.

"Well," she said, "I enjoyed skating so much that when I told my parents that all I wanted to do was skate for the rest of my life, they told me that it wasn't a job that someone could do and earn a living—that is to make money. My father told me that I could skate all I wanted but only as a hobby. Skating was not something that would put food on the table when I was a grownup. My parents told me that people always would need nurses or teachers. So, I decided to become a teacher instead, because that's what I understood girls did when I was growing up."

I loved story time and especially hearing about real people's stories. I had no great interest listening to typical happily-ever-after stories about princesses hidden in castles or pumpkins turning into carriages. Those stories did not seem real to me. But when I heard about a person's life, it inspired and moved me. Just like the moment with my teacher that day.

As I listened to her speak, I thought how sad it was that skating was not an acceptable thing to do. Especially when it was so exciting.

Why did her parents have to decide what she could do in her life, I wondered? It didn't seem fair. I noticed that Ms. McDonald's energy got more animated the more she spoke about her dream of being a champion skater, and sadder when she talked about her parents deciding on her life path.

That was my first awareness that it was possible for childhood dreams to turn into a lifelong profession. It was also my first exposure to the feeling of one's power of choice being taken away. What I struggled in my young mind to comprehend was how others could decide how your life would turn out and what you would do in it.

That kindergarten moment also gave me my first experience in seeing how taking on other people's beliefs and not honoring one's own desires and dreams could shape one's life forever.

Stereotypes

My family was considered traditional. My father, Nick, worked a blue-collar job and was the breadwinner. He had immigrated to Canada in the 1950s, leaving his family behind in the Ukraine. Upon settling in Northern Ontario, a province in Eastern Canada, he took a job in the copper mining industry as an electrician and had a secure nine-to-five lifestyle.

My mother, Anna, whom he met at a church social, gave up her dreams of a career in nursing to stay home and raise her two children. Her parents, my grandparents, Maria and Ivan, lived down the road from us. And my aunts and uncles, my mother's siblings, were also close by. I had a much older brother, Peter. By the time I came along—a completely unexpected event, I was told—he was starting to pursue his own interests. As I was growing up, Peter kept much to himself and seemed constantly annoyed that he had a much younger sister. I felt like an only child. And in many ways, I was.

I spent much of my time alone. There weren't many children who lived on our street. So I developed my own form of play, entertaining myself. My friends consisted mostly of the invisible kind, as well as the multitude of creatures in nature—ant hills, dragonflies, birds, and the big blue sky.

Although my mother had abandoned her education and potential career to get married and raise a family, she considered education important for her children. Education, according to her, was the key for getting a job and making money. Good grades were important; they opened doors to post-secondary education and that was what got you the security of the job.

Ah yes, but this was also the early 1970s. In my family, strict gender roles dominated. We were considered a minority—Ukrainian, an Eastern European culture where patriarchal roles still existed. The man was considered the head of the household and the monetary provider. The woman got married, became a housewife, and was expected to be a mother. Careers outside of the home were not an option for women.

And although the importance of education was a consistent theme throughout my early and adolescent years, very different types of careers were encouraged for my brother than for me. My mother often repeated the story that my brother at the age of five knew that he wanted to be a doctor. He was encouraged to go to university; in fact, he entered post-secondary education to pursue a career in medicine at sixteen, when many young people are still trying to figure out which direction they are heading and how soon they can get their driver's licenses.

I, on the other hand, was not encouraged in any specific direction other than the basics—science, math, and English. These were considered tickets to my future, I was told over and over. "Someday, you never know when you will need to use these," my mother would chant repeatedly.

I could take typing and shorthand, because, according to my family, this could net me a wonderful job as a secretary. However, the only thing that held my interest were the creative arts—music, drawing, painting, writing, reading, and even chemistry, where I could create something and watch it blow up. What I know now is that my mother's feelings about girls' roles were tainted by her own unhappiness in her marriage and stemmed from her own dreams being quashed by her father, my grandfather Ivan.

My grandfather was a quiet, yet strict man. A stocky, broadly built Ukrainian, he had strict views and beliefs on life. He was deeply religious, coming from an Orthodox faith. He married Maria, my grandmother, who was Polish Catholic. Family and church were everything to him—traditional roles, traditional values, strong work ethic. My grandparents immigrated to Canada from the Ukraine sometime after the war and settled briefly in Saskatchewan and Alberta. They were farmers, determined to make a life for themselves and their growing family.

Eventually the lure of good, secure jobs at the booming smelters and metal mines had them making their way to Northern Ontario where my grandparents settled and put down roots. They would stay there for the rest of their lives. My mother and three siblings grew up in Ontario, and were considered to be a good, solid European family. Such was my heritage.

I always enjoyed spending time with my grandfather Ivan. There is always someone in your family that you bond with more closely than others. My grandfather was the first person that I remember in my life with whom I had that strong connection. I did not know him very well as a person, and only later would learn of his history, his beliefs, and how they led to my shaping as a person. Still, somehow I had an unspoken bond with this man.

Even though he was a chain-smoker and ultimately would lose his life to emphysema, as a six-year-old, I enjoyed his company immensely. He was a quiet, unassuming man, and although I would never see him show affection to anyone else, he would always receive me into his lap for a cuddle and a hug. It was at least thirty years after his death that I discovered that he, in part, was integral in my mother's unhappiness, which impacted on mine. Isn't it funny how beliefs carry through generation and even after that generation? And it's awful when they continue on without anyone stopping the reenactment.

Before my mother married my father, she lived in the United States, far from home. She chose to leave the family home to experience life. After all, what young person, living in a small community, would not want to venture out into the world and experience all that it had to offer? She completed nursing school, had a job, and had begun her career.

But my grandfather did not believe in women having jobs. His view was that it was a woman's duty to get married, have children, and take on the traditional role of a housewife. Their lives, according to him, were planned out. In fact, both my mother and aunt's lives were centered on marriage and children, while my uncles' careers were perfectly acceptable when they became teachers and lawyers.

Children naturally do things to please their parents, especially when they are young. The first step toward self-actualization is going through the process of winning approval from one's immediate environment. Parents are the strongest model for that, and my mother was no exception. To please her father, my mother abandoned her job, her career, a potential marriage to a non-Ukrainian man, and dutifully came back home to Northern Ontario. And as they say, the rest is history. I am living proof of that choice.

However, it was immensely clear, especially in my teenage years, that her life was full of struggle. Her own demons didn't help; she battled alcoholism and prescription drug addiction, perhaps as an escape from dealing with her own pain and unresolved issues with her father. Even with her dreams and desires dashed, somewhere deep within her and in her own way, I believe she tried her best to pass on a ray of hope of following one's own heart.

She constantly reminded me that it was important to achieve an education, but as "something to fall back on," in case relationships did not work out. When I was old enough to comprehend the gravity of that statement, it felt like a death sentence.

Needless to say, I learned many lessons early in life—to detect what did not feel right within me, to differentiate other people's beliefs from mine, and most importantly, to listen to my inner nudging when it came to choosing and designing my own life path. Because, you see, I believe that one's life purpose always shows itself early on. All too often, though, other people's views, especially familial or societal, end up being piled on top. In the end, the early signs that hold potential for greatness wind up buried, only to show up much later in midlife, when we are dissatisfied with our jobs, our relationships, our lives, and we start searching for something to give us meaning.

If only those childhood dreams could be taken seriously, without other people's beliefs and expectations being imposed on them…if only.

And That's Who I Am

So there I was, Olena, Anna and Nick's daughter, Maria and Ivan's granddaughter. I looked exactly like my father—long brown hair with ringlets, big brown eyes, big smile. I looked every inch the little princess. My mother loved to dress me up as a doll. Because I was so tiny when I was born, I did wear doll clothes briefly, because standard-sized baby clothes didn't fit. My mother had fixed ideas about what was appropriate clothing for a girl—dresses, skirts below the knee, buttoned-up shirts to the neck, and sturdy walking shoes.

Those were the kinds of clothes I wore, and I disliked them immensely. It bothered me that I could not choose what I wanted to wear. To this day, although I tolerate dressing up once in a while, I am most comfortable in what I feel most comfortable wearing, and that changes on a daily basis. There are truly some advantages of becoming an adult!

English was not my first language. Ukrainian was the only language spoken at home. However, because my mother stressed the importance of education, and because I was a quick learner, I learned to read, write, and speak both Ukrainian and English before I was five. Funny thing, though, I spoke English with a lisp. The Ukrainian language is unusual, with its Cyrillic alphabet and musical tones. Many of the consonants are soft and rolled, which gave me a distinctive accent. A keen five-year-old on my first day of kindergarten asked me why I spoke so funny and what kind of a name I had. That was just the beginning of my distinctiveness.

Not long after I started in the grand halls of Lansdowne Elementary School in Sudbury, Ontario, I was considered a problem. Not only did my funny little lisp have to go, but I spent most of my days in kindergarten not getting involved in what the other children were doing. Both my mother and the teacher thought that it was because of my speech. I was self-conscious about my lisp and my accent. I didn't, however, think at any time that I had a problem. I figured that was just who I was.

I was promptly enrolled in speech therapy classes. The teachers thought it was improper to have rolled *r*'s and not the hard ones common in the English language. It seems my mouth just had a lot of trouble converting from one to the other between leaving home and arriving at school.

I was pulled from my class every week to a sit in a separate room with a prim and professional looking woman, who was described as my speech therapist, and who was there to "help me correct my problem." She made me practice correctly placed *r*'s, so that my reading and communication would be "acceptable" to the powers that be. Needless to say, I decided that I was going to jump through the hoops and acquiesce, as I knew it would get me out of those classes faster. I was happy when speech therapy ended. But it definitely wouldn't be the last time that I was singled out.

Life Purpose Comes Early

Despite my supposed communication adversities, reading and writing were among my strengths. I was fascinated by words from the moment I could walk and talk. As a young child, I devoured books, especially on the topics of crystals and stones; magical stories about unicorns, fairies, and leprechauns; stories with purpose and depth; mysteries; biographies; and the esoteric. While other little children dumped sand repeatedly out of dump trucks in kindergarten, I sat in a rocking chair behind stacks of books, engrossed in my own little world— reading.

I strongly identified with characters in books or on television who had special talents and gifts, like Samantha on *Bewitched*, Mister Ed the talking horse, and Jeannie on *I Dream of Jeannie*.

I wanted to be like the heroes and heroines of the day who hid their identities. I surrounded myself with the likes of Wonder Woman, Batman, Superman, and Spiderman, champions of the underdogs. I knew deep down that they were different, just like me, even though I didn't know in what way I differed. I often wondered how it was that someone grew up to know what they were meant to do in their life. It all seemed so exciting to live a life fully knowing who you were.

When I wasn't pretending that I was capturing villains with my magical spider web that emerged from my wrists or twirling around like a hurricane as I was transforming into Wonder Woman, I would spend my time sitting in front of a typewriter, pretending that I was writing books.

Another pivotal moment in self-awakening came in that same kindergarten class. While teachers worried about my apparent lack of interest in getting my hands dirty in the paint pots, I gravitated toward a battered, old, unused typewriter that sat isolated near the front door of my class.

It was while sitting in front of the lonely old typewriter that I remember most distinctly, how great it made me feel. Even though I technically did not know what I was typing or even how to type, I enjoyed the feel of my hands on the keys. I loved to see lots of black marks on the white page. And I thought it was great that I was getting to write stories all on my own, not just to read them.

Amidst the children screaming, running, laughing, and making loud noises as the Tonka trucks turned into gigantic monsters emptying sand into the pit, I had a pivotal moment, although I didn't consciously know it at the time.

When a newspaper reporter came into my class to do a feature on children and play, I'm sure it must have seemed odd to him see a six-year-old sitting with her hands on the keys, not showing any interest in dump trucks full of sand. I guess that was a magnet for the reporter, because it was so out of the ordinary. So there it was, my first interview. And in stereotypical, adult fashion, the reporter asked me what I wanted to do when I grew up. I nonchalantly told the nice gentleman that I was busy—busy writing my book. When queried on what my book was about, I politely answered that it was "all about me."

Even though over the next thirty years I would have many nudgings along the path, it took me many attempts to finally come to the realization that one's purpose in life truly shows itself early in life, as do the gifts that come along with it.

Altered Realities

CHAPTER THREE

Intentions count in your actions.[3]

—Abu Bakr
First Muslim leader after Muhammad

I spent much of my early childhood wondering just how normal I really was. After all, like many of the children in school, I grew up in the era of *Wonder Woman*, *Star Trek*, and the *Six Million Dollar Man*, where all the "ordinary" heroes possessed extraordinary powers.

Barely out of elementary school, I was mesmerized by biblical figures and spiritual teachers such as Jesus. I marveled at the miracles performed by this awesome man who walked this earth so long ago.

Since I was often left alone to play, I spent countless hours pretending that I had these powerful abilities. I would stare intensely at something, locking my eyes on an object, willing it to move or thinking that I could actually have light rays shooting out of my eyes. I would run around and spin rapidly in circles, pretending to turn into a super-being.

Often, I would turn the bed sheets into a makeshift cape and make the bed a jumping off point for flying. It seemed to me such a natural thing to do! I would also pretend that I could make objects move or bend just by pointing a finger at them or focusing on them with my mind.

Undeterred by the lack of movement, I was convinced many times over that this would happen—I just had to keep working at it. Sad to say, my "walking on water" experiment was reluctantly abandoned when I fell into the bathtub with a great splash and nearly cracked my skull on the ceramic tile.

But the interesting thing was, I enjoyed these adventures. They held a great fascination for me—and they were fun. I truly believed that I not only had these magical powers, but that they were something I could use for the rest of my life.

My imagination was not that out of line. Looking back on my childhood, there were many occasions when I know that my imaginary friends that I talked and listened to were actually angels, spirits, and occasionally little creatures such as fairies.

As early as age six, I recall having visions of spirits and beings. Brightly colored lights would dance around me, flashing out of the corners of my eyes, always accompanied by a warm, fuzzy feeling. Some lights glowed white and had wings, and some wore soft-colored robes. I knew instinctively that they were angels. Most of the time, they would appear at night, hanging around my bed, never saying anything, just being there in their loving energy.

Today, I know when the angels are around me. I still receive the warm, fuzzy feelings like a cloak, and I see them clearly and in detail with my mind's eye. I will talk more about the chakras and the third eye later in this book.

Nighttime was my favorite time. I loved going to sleep in my bed. I must have been one of the few children on the planet who couldn't wait for bedtime, for that was when the party started for me!

When I closed my eyes, it was as if I entered another realm—an addictive realm, in a sense. I wanted to close my eyes all the time. Behind them lay the most vivid pictures imaginable. I would see animals, people, and faces, especially children, and they would speak to me. For you see, behind my eyes, there also lay a safe haven that I could go into whenever I wanted.

Eventually, I discovered that I could access this secret world behind my eyes in the daytime. It was a world that felt peaceful, loving, and safe. I believed that everything in nature had wings and was angelic, from the four-legged animals to the winged butterflies to the blades of grass around me.

While our home was small, the backyard was huge. I loved to run around in the fresh green grass and feel the earth against my body. It was on this immense patch of grass that I would often lie on my back in the summertime, staring up at the sunshine. I loved the feeling of soaking up the light rays through my eyes and then shutting them tightly. The tighter I squeezed, the clearer I believed that I could see what lay behind them.

I would play games with myself, testing to see with each squeeze how much bigger and better the vision could be. Often after such a tight squeeze, I would open my eyes to look at the trees or flowers and see tiny sparks of light jumping from petal to petal. I later discovered that these were fairies, and as they appeared to me, tiny beings of light with little wings.

The other world always felt loving and safe, and the beings in those realms became my invisible friends and regular companions. I knew that I was never alone, whether I was walking back and forth from school or playing by myself in my backyard. My companions were always with me. Whenever I needed a friend, I turned to them, summoning them silently within my mind.

I never discounted any of these experiences. In fact, I truly believed that everyone else saw what I saw and experienced what I experienced. To a young child, beyond the realm of reason, occurrences like these are normal, unless the external world says otherwise. To me, I was a true knower of angels, fairies, pixies, and anything magical. Instead of merely reading books about them, I found that I experienced them, and to a young girl, that was just grand.

It never occurred to me that others around me didn't experience similar things. Little did I know that life as I knew it would be changed into what seemed to be the worst period of my life. And it was the safe haven of angels and spirit beings that I would eventually rely on for my survival in the physical world

I am a firm believer that all children are psychic. Not only that, I believe that we are all born with that inherent ability. It is our birthright. The difference with Indigo children, however, is that many of them exhibit this at an early age in all its forms. They are not just clairvoyant but tend to have astute clairaudience (clear hearing) and clairsentience (clear feeling). To them, such experiences are normal, and the knowledge that others do not or cannot experience similar situations falls into their definition of abnormal.

Grounded in five-sensory practice, adults often logically discount these abilities as childhood imagination or simply a phase that will be outgrown. By the time children reach the age of seven to nine, a crucial development phase, they tend to forget their spiritual connections. It is at this crucial time in children's lives that this inherent ability can easily be squashed or suppressed.

Talents & Altered States

When I was six years old, my mother enrolled me in music classes at the local Catholic high school in Sudbury, Ontario. My brother, Peter, nine years older than

I, would often play the piano in our home. Music ran in my family. My mother and her siblings often sang or played instruments. Like many children, I would mimic my older brother, tapping out the tunes that he had just played. I displayed an early talent for accurately playing back whatever had just been played. I could hear it, and without knowing exactly what keys I was pressing, could reproduce it perfectly. My mother decided that I had a natural, musical ear. Since musicians ran in my family, she took it upon herself to foster that talent in me.

The school was large and imposing, set up high on a hill and quite a fair walk from our home. We had only one car, and no buses ran in my area of town. So we walked everywhere. By the time my mother and I reached the school, we were usually breathless, and fairly often I was too tired to start anything new.

Physical fatigue aside, I approached my classes with apprehension. I didn't know what to expect and was somewhat fearful. The music school was part of a Catholic all-girls school. Most of the teachers were nuns and lived in a convent attached to the back of the school.

Sister Victoria was my first music teacher. She was an older, pleasant woman and did not wear the usual nun's habit. As I sat nervously in a large room with about twenty other children, surrounded by keyboards, I wondered what I was doing there. All I wanted to do was play music. I wasn't sure what being in that room with other children was going to accomplish.

But pretty soon I got involved in the ins and outs of learning how to master the piano. Sister Victoria was a firm but polite teacher. Each week, I would take the long walk from my home, trudging up the big hill to sit in her class to learn notes, read music, and listen to her tell stories about her days as a concert violinist in the symphony orchestra.

Because cultural heritage was important to my family, my mother insisted that I immerse myself in the Ukrainian arts—such as dancing, cooking, language, handiwork, and painting. So around the same time as music lessons began, I found myself with a very busy schedule. I was attracted to any expressive art form and particularly enjoyed dancing. Moving my body was freeing, and I was enchanted by the colorful costumes that I got to wear. I loved it so much that ballet and tap were added to my growing list of lessons.

I excelled in both school and my extracurricular activities. After a while, however, I became bored with the structure of the lessons. I found it tedious to continuously repeat the many mechanical aspects of learning either an instrument or the many steps involved in learning to dance.

I did enjoy school and was a quick learner. By the time I reached first grade, I had mastered two languages—written and spoken. It was difficult for me to sit there listening to others learning the alphabet when I was already reading books and zipping through the material in no time flat. I was subjected to numerous proficiency tests, because my teacher had decided that I should not attend the group classes, since I was not learning anything. I spent most of my time either helping other children in the class with their letters or off by myself reading, because I had zipped through the homework early.

The logistics of learning art forms was, as well, too tedious and unstimulating. My dance teachers noticed my boredom and recommended to my mother that I be bumped up in my classes and receive focused, individualized instruction, especially in music. Apparently I displayed a great talent and was labeled as gifted.

All of my teachers thought I had a flair for performance. I was actually a very shy child and preferred to stay away from public performances. To help me overcome that, I was immersed in competitions, recitals, and any opportunity to be in the public eye that crossed my path. Performing assumed a prominent place in my life for the next fifteen years.

To this day, whenever I speak to groups or teach classes, I am thankful for the many years of training and experience that I have had from dancing, playing, and speaking in public. It molded me and helped me learn how to become comfortable with crowds.

Within the space of six months, my life accelerated tenfold. I was bumped from first grade one to third grade in the middle of a year and was pulled out of group music and dance lessons. I was not a happy camper. I was the youngest and smallest child in my class at school, and I missed the friends that I had to leave behind. I was thrust into a situation where all the children were two years older, much larger, and very curious about that "gifted" child who had entered their space.

I was perceived as different. And I felt different. I did not belong. I didn't feel like I fit in anywhere. In fact, I did not know how to fit in, where or how to start. I was the foreign, extremely shy kid with glasses and braces. I was small, leggy, and thin; my clothes and hair were out of style. I had a strange name that no one seemed able to pronounce—and I was smart. I was nicknamed Rapunzel, because I had extremely long hair that reached down my back. I had near-perfect grades; school was easy for me. But I felt both embarrassed and ashamed for being smart, for speaking a different language, and for how I looked. I just wanted to be normal, like the children I had left behind in first grade. At one point, I prayed to God to make me less intelligent, just to feel like I could fit in somewhere. That didn't happen. Instead, all of those things became strong and automatic strikes against me—a girl to be picked on.

I became very self-conscious from that point onward, lasting until I left high school and moved away from home. The more self-conscious I became, the more I was on the receiving end of taunts, teasing, and bullying by many children. Some of them got quite mean in their tactics. Several of the older boys in my classes took it upon themselves to start following me outside of class, trying to prevent me from walking safely home after school. They hid behind cars and threw things at me like snowballs, or worse, rotten vegetables. My visits to the principal's office to complain about these offenders became a weekly occurrence. Each day quickly turned into a nightmare.

At a time when a child should be learning healthy self-esteem and becoming secure within herself, I was starting to live in fear and walk on eggshells. There was no such thing as the anti-bullying laws we have today. Teachers did not take situations like that very seriously. I started to lose trust in people—trust in my teachers, the administrators, and the other children. I found it difficult to make friends, because everyone I got to know seemed to want to stay away from me, because they were afraid to be associated with the "kid who got picked on" and didn't want to be targeted themselves.

Every night when I went to bed, I would pray to God to take me away from all of this and to make all the bullies go away. I figured the louder I was in my head, the better God could hear me and the faster he would act. I even had episodic anger toward God, telling him that he really needed to fix all of this—or else. *How could he let a little kid suffer?* I would cry out in my mind. I desperately wanted everything to disappear. But it didn't, at least not as I hoped.

I would close my eyes many nights, willing the situations to change, thinking to myself that my mind was so powerful that all I had to do was will it all to go away. I could think that everything would be different, and it would be. Little did I know that I was tapping into my greater sense of self and learning the art of manifestation, simply by changing my thoughts around the situation. It was at this time that I consciously turned more and more of my sights to God and the unseen.

I began noticing that the worse I felt about myself, the worse the incidents got. There had to be a connection. Even though I now understand that my lack of self-esteem at that time was like a magnet to the other children who took it upon themselves to taunt and tease me, back then I didn't understand the extent of what "asking for it" really meant.

"They're actually scared of you," the guidance counselor Mrs. LePage would tell me, on the many trips that I took to her office.

"How could these kids be scared of me?" I wondered aloud.

"Olena," she would say, "you threaten them—you're different, you're smart, and you don't do what they do. Usually anyone who picks on someone else is really scared inside, but they cover it up by pretending that they are loud, big, and tough. And another reason they target you is that you show them that you're scared. They see that, and it gives them a reason to continue." Her wise words struck a chord long and deep within me.

I carefully considered this. Perhaps there was something to the power of my thoughts. Perhaps, just perhaps, if I could start looking at these people in a different way and seeing them as having a scared little child inside of them, I could feel differently toward them. And if I started to feel differently toward them, I would potentially start to feel differently about myself.

Now in my thirties, I am fully aware that how we perceive ourselves and how we come across does truly show up in our environment. Our perceptions affect how other people perceive us. I think it's valuable to teach that to our children when they are young, so that they can learn how to come from a place of empowerment, rather than disempowerment.

It was an eye-opening experience for me and a major shift in consciousness in how I approached life. After all, seeing myself as a victim for a long time didn't appeal to me. In fact, it got dull and boring running to the teachers and the principal all the time "telling" on these boys. I started to feel that I was engaging in behavior just like they were, and that the teachers were getting tired of me coming to them. I could almost hear them in my head, wishing that they didn't have to deal with a kid who was constantly being bullied. The sad part, I realized, was that those boys didn't know how to handle it either. So, it was up to me and only me.

On top of my school challenges, my home environment was not fairing too well at this period of my life. My parents were unhappy in their marriage. I didn't know it at the time, but my mother chose to deal with her unhappiness and disintegrating relationship through alcohol and a never-ending supply of prescription drugs.

My father became distant to me. I hardly saw him. He would come home from work late and disappear into his workshop. By the time he would come into the house, I was asleep. As this routine continued for a few years, my mother started to become more and more aggressive. She was always fairly strict and demanding, but the silent workings of alcohol and medications started to have an effect on her mood and reactions, especially toward me.

As an adult and mother myself, I can only imagine how she struggled to cope with the knowledge that her relationship was falling apart, while raising two children, one of whom was about to leave home. My mother lived very much under the scrutiny of her family, her religion, and the small cultural community in which we lived. To her, a failing relationship reflected on her own sense of failure as a person, a wife, a mother, and a daughter. It was something that she had great difficulty dealing with, and so turned to external substances to escape the pain and disappointment she felt inside of herself.

When I was eight, my parents separated. My father moved out of the house, and right on his heels, my brother left home, headed for college. I saw my brother sporadically over the years, but I would be seventeen years old before I saw my father again.

My mother and I were left alone in the house. Due to the separation, she had to find work to support us. I ended up spending a lot of time with my grandmother, who would come early in the morning to watch me and see me off to school. Eventually, the expenses were too great, and the legalities of the separation forced my mother to sell our family home. Soon after that we moved up the street into my grandmother's home—my grandfather had long since passed away. My mother would often refer to this time as the time everybody abandoned her—her husband, her son, and her father, now deceased. More and more, she started to take her frustrations out on me, physically, emotionally, and mentally.

I believe her sense of failure really kicked in at this time. Having to swallow her pride and move in with her elderly mother made it much worse. Her moods started to flip-flop. Her constant complaining about being a victim became quite stressful for me. Though the pattern of alcoholism ran in my family, this period seemed to trigger her heavier alcohol usage.

I was in a situation with no father, no brother, and, basically, no male members of the household. I was at a crucial time when male models were important in a child's life, and I ended up then (and for a long time after that) not knowing what that was like.

I turned much of my energy into my schoolwork and my artistic activities, especially music. For a while, I maintained excellent grades and excelled in music. I started to become involved more and more in performing.

Even though I disliked the drudgery of practicing, I discovered that when I immersed myself in the sounds of the music or the movements of my dance, I entered an almost altered state of mind. It was like walking into another world, which felt wonderful. When I was engrossed in music, I was able to shut out all the stressful, awful events that were happening around me. And with performances on stage, came the need to learn to memorize music and dance steps. Memorization to me involved visualization, being able to see in my mind's eye the sheets of music or the performance of a dance as if it were right in front of me.

To briefly explain the concept of visualization, it is the art of creating mental images. Mental images have a powerful effect on our bodies and minds. Perhaps you have heard of athletes, or musicians, or others who spend time visualizing their performances before actually putting them into physical action. Evidence shows that when you visualize a task, it becomes easier to do. When you visualize what you would like to see happening, it creates a strong, realistic imprint in the mind, sending positive messages to the subconscious and helping change any negative or unwanted messages that exist. This visual imprint brings the actual event or activity that much closer to physical reality.

Both my mother and my teachers came to the conclusion that I was performer material, and I ended up being groomed as a budding concert pianist. I did not necessarily see this at the time as a career or something that I would do for the rest of my life, but it was obviously something for which I had a gift. One of the gifts that I had that all my teachers discovered was the ability to visualize. Just like my earlier days visualizing myself being a superhero or willing the blades of grass to move by staring intently at them, I was able to shift into this space quickly and easily whenever I sat down to play or dance.

I learned that this was an unlimited realm. One could visualize anything and everything. What became consciously more and more apparent to me was the growing power of mental imagery and intention that I had at my disposal. I started using this constantly and purposefully. Before every music or dance competition, my teachers would coach me on seeing the music in front of me as I played, seeing my fingers pressing the right keys, tapping into the feeling of the music, my feet taking the right steps, and ultimately, picturing myself winning.

It paid off. I won awards, placing first in almost every competition I entered. I ended up playing with the local symphony orchestra.

I used these powers of visualization in school to study for tests, before speaking in front of the class, and even against the dreaded teasing and taunting from classmates. Visualization became an integral part of my life and served as a major escape from the emotional upheavals everywhere else.

Between the challenges at school and the growing stress and challenges at home, the wonderful realm where visualization existed became a lifeline for me, one on which I relied more and more. While I knew that I could not control what other people did, I started realizing that I could create my own reality, just by seeing it in my mind. Looking back, it was one of the many tools that I used to survive these difficult years.

I See Angels, God, and Dead People

CHAPTER FOUR

No one can give a definition of the soul.
But we know what it feels like.
The soul is the sense of something higher than ourselves,
something that stirs in us thoughts, hopes, and aspirations
which go out to the world of goodness, truth, and beauty.
The soul is a burning desire to breathe in this world of light and
never to lose it, to remain children of light.[4]

—Albert Schweitzer
German-Alsatian philosopher and theologian

From an early age I had a strong awareness of heaven, angels, saints, and God. Most of it came from the fact that my family was very religious, with beliefs deeply steeped in saints, prayer, ceremony, ritual, and consistent church attendance. I was immersed in it from the very moment of being here. It was with my religious upbringing where I started questioning what was true or not for me, as well as experiencing phenomena that didn't fall into the realm of acceptability of the religious structure into which I was born.

My community was like a village. Everybody of the same ethnic clan knew each other, talked about each other, and either met at church or socialized outside of it. Religion and church were the central part of not only my family's life, but of most people who emigrated from other parts of the world.

The general premise of my church upbringing was that people must be God-fearing. God the Almighty had immense power to love as well as to punish. The belief that you had to "be good or else God would punish you" was prevalent in the church that I regularly attended and became the driving force of my childhood programming. Being "good" included attending Sunday church services, not taking the Lord's name in vain, and religiously following the Ten Commandments. Heaven forbid should lightning and thunder occur, for surely they were signs of God's wrath.

Church was not one of my favorite places to be, especially for worship. Being from the Ukrainian Orthodox faith, I attended a Ukrainian Greek Orthodox church. For those not familiar with Eastern European religious institutions, the physical structures are usually massive and imposing and built unlike most churches that you see today. Typical Orthodox churches are ornate and grandiose on the inside as well as the outside. The smell of incense, the icons and stained glass adorning the walls, and the rich, warm colors made you feel like you were in a royal household.

Certain childhood experiences are hardwired into our adult consciousness. To this day, even though I declare myself to be nonreligious and a nonchurchgoer, the smell of incense and light refracting and reflecting off stained glass resonates with my inner being. But aside from my appreciation of some of the symbols of religion, my childhood interest in attending church was nonexistent; I had no desire to repeat the words or to be "seen."

As a child, I could never comprehend the purpose of attending church. I couldn't understand why for two short hours, once a week, all the same people got dressed in nice clothing, came to this one big building, sat in the same pews and the same seats, verbalized the same dialogue, sang the same songs, and then went home, only to gossip and speak negatively about other people the other six and a half days of the week.

On top of that, the fundamental patriarchal beliefs of the Orthodox Church produced strict gender rules. It was forbidden for a woman to be a clergyperson. No female minister existed in the Greek Orthodox religion. Within the church structure, the ministers' area within the church was walled off from the congregation. No females were allowed to walk beyond the pulpit into that walled-off area. Males, however, were allowed access from the moment a baby boy was baptized. During a typical baptismal ceremony it was standard procedure to "introduce" the male baby to the church by carrying him through all parts of it, including the "forbidden zone," as I called it.

What made matters worse in my mind was that both the men and women chose to segregate themselves within the church. It was not uncommon for the women to sit on one side, and the men on the other.

Having the stubborn, rebellious nature of an Indigo, I naturally went against these rules. There was an inherent knowing that the rigidity of the rules and beliefs spoke to inequality, unfairness, and the unjustness of human behavior. So I deliberately sat on the "male side" of the congregation, sneaked into the pastor's area out of curiosity (only to discover nothing of importance lay behind those walls), and boldly argued with anyone who crossed my path as to the non-efficacy of having only male clergy and to the gender inequality within baptismal rituals.

I constantly questioned the purpose of attending church, only to be met with a look of horror as if I had uttered the most blasphemous of statements. I got the pat answer: "Because that's where you go to talk to God."

That sounded so wrong to me. According to the beliefs of the church, God was something never to be seen, something we would never be allowed to see.

Allowed? Did we need permission to see God? And whose permission did we need?

My reasoning was that if God was the creator of the Universe, of all things "seen and unseen," that meant that everything I looked at, touched, smelled, or tasted—even me—was a part of that creation.

If God created the flowers, the animals, the grass, the sky, and especially the people, then wasn't God everywhere I looked?

Moreover, the orthodox faith believed in the Triune God, comprised of God, Jesus Christ, and the Holy Spirit. One could only pray to God through the medium of Jesus Christ, as Jesus was the intermediary between the humans and the unseen God. No one ever had a good explanation as to what the Holy Spirit really was, and I couldn't comprehend the difference between seeing or talking to God versus talking to Jesus Christ or the Holy Spirit. To me it was all one and the same.

And neither of them was any harder than the other to communicate with in my experience. Needless to say, when I got up the courage to speak up one day and said that I could talk to God while taking a walk in the forest or even while sitting in the bathtub, it was just too much for my family and the parish priest. I was told that my comments were utterly ridiculous, and that I was too young to know what I was talking about. After that, I kept my own knowing and opinions to myself.

As much as my family and the culture were trying to mold me by the rituals and rules of the church, I believed that God and the Universe were far more expansive than that. The church was far too limiting for me, and it did not seem realistic. I found it difficult to believe that God only existed inside the four walls of the church and only on Sundays. The teachings also said that no one could speak to God, other than the "special" or "chosen" ones, such as the ministers or clergy of the higher orders like the Pope of the Catholic faith. Ordinary citizens like me were limited in these abilities.

Instead of acquiescing to these beliefs, this prompted me to start asking questions and demanding answers—and ironically, throwing them mentally up to God.

I want to see you, God. Please talk to me. If you are really there, please prove to me that you are really there. Show yourself!

As a child, I didn't see anything wrong with the request.

A response to my pleas came quickly. As I have already mentioned, nighttime was my favorite time. I loved going to bed, because I got to see a lot of activity going on behind my eyes. Nighttime was like a gateway that I could walk through into another realm, and as I got older it was a welcome escape from 3-D reality.

I remember one night lying in my bed, bundled up in my blankets. My mother and I had moved into my grandmother's house, and my bedroom was in the attic. It was somewhat private, cozy, and quiet, like a sanctuary to me.

That day had been trying. I hadn't adjusted to moving away from the home that I knew, my mother was on an emotional rampage, and I had had a bad day at school. I was sad, lonely, and unable to understand how to handle the changes that had taken place in my life. And I had no one to talk to about my feelings. I gratefully buried myself under the blankets and cried quietly to myself, hiding my sounds so no one would hear me. I didn't want to anger my mother any further or trigger any other adverse reactions toward me.

As I lay there facing the ceiling, the blankets covering my tear-stained face, I begged God to take me away.

I want to go home God. I want to go home to heaven. I hate it here, and I don't want to be here. Please take me away from this horrible place, I cried silently.

I visualized pictures, much like the 3-D icons in the church, of angels gently picking me up and whisking me off away from Earth and into the clouds.

Suddenly, I felt my body turn rigid, as if a powerful force had come over me and pinned me down to the bed. Through my tears and my sadness, I looked up at the ceiling and saw the face of Jesus, just like the icon in our former home when

I was little. It was hovering in front of me, and the energy was powerful, bright, full of light, and extremely loving and peaceful.

I was mesmerized by this, and as I continued to lock eyes with the figure of Jesus, I felt something else. It had no form that I could put into words, but it was distinctive enough that I knew what it was. I felt a hand descend from somewhere above me and place itself, palm facing downward, on my chest. It was warm, enveloped my whole body, and made me feel like I was immersed in a bubble of light. I felt like I was being taken in a parent's arms and cradled. I loved the feeling of safety, security, and comfort that it brought me. Words can't fully describe the event and feelings. But above all, I had no fear, perhaps because I was young and open to all these experiences. Instinctively I knew that this was the hand of God.

This experience forever changed my perception of the unseen. To me, this was real, and any doubts that I had had about God were wiped out in that moment. I believe that this was the beginning of my awareness of my own intuitive and psychic abilities, and the beginning of the knowledge of turning inward to God instead of looking outside of myself when I needed help.

Meeting the Other Side

As time went on, I began to have many precognitive experiences and visions. When I was young, it was common for me to have unseen companions. I fully believe that a young child's energy is very open and accepting, and many of the invisible friends that they spend time with are actually angels, and other beings in spirit, including ones that have passed over.

I noticed that my invisible companions would start talking to me, and I could hear what they were saying much more clearly than I did before. I also became aware of my feelings and how my feelings changed when I was confronted with a negative situation versus a positive one. After my experience with the hand of God, my visuals changed as well. At first, I thought perhaps it was due to the practice of memorizing pages of music and strengthening my visual muscles. But there was more.

The concept of being "taken away to heaven" fascinated me. I started wondering what heaven was, what happened when someone was dying, and what happened after they died. Since the Bible was important in our family, and I was made to read it as a child, I was particularly drawn to the New Testament and stories about Jesus Christ, especially stories of specific miracles about raising people from the dead. I wondered how that was possible and *what dead people really looked like.*

Until I spoke out and described what I believed to be true (only to get chided for having blasphemous thoughts), I truly thought that these visions were normal occurrences. Well, that did not last long.

I had my first glimpses into the doorway of the other side early in 1973. I was in the hospital, suffering from a serious bout of pneumonia and tonsillitis. As a young child, born prematurely, I had never fully developed my immune system. Physically, I was never strong and was frequently sick with childhood illnesses and colds. It was easy for me to get sick. I was forever in and out of hospitals and doctors' offices. I had asthma as a child and was often wheezing or having periodic breathing difficulties.

On this occasion, I had the flu, which lead to a high fever and eventually pneumonia—and an emergency rush to the hospital. Once my breathing was under control, I had an operation to remove my tonsils. I couldn't eat anything and was told by the nurses that I would have difficulty speaking for a while. The room that I was in was not isolated. I shared the room with a little girl named Susie.

Susie was an interesting little spirit, very animated and talkative and intrigued with having another person sharing *her* space. My mother had brought some toys that I kept tucked away in the hospital nightstand. In particular I had a plastic snap necklace made up of individual multicolored letters that I could take apart and snap together to make different words. Susie loved playing with my toys, but I was not always willing to share. I was frustrated that my voice was no more than a whisper, and I had difficulty getting out of bed and running around the room, because I was still recuperating from pneumonia. As if reading my thoughts, Susie would tell me that she had been in the hospital for a very long time. Her hospital room had a little closet, which had some of her clothes, and her nightstand was filled with books and other toys. It certainly seemed like a place she knew all too well. Not a shy girl whatsoever and no doubt compensating for my inability to speak, Susie told me that her body was ill, and she too had had an operation. Unlike my tonsil removal, the doctors, she said, had removed "something bad" inside of her body. Her blood was "sick," Susie mentioned, and she told me that she had to take a lot of medicine to help her get better.

As she spoke, I remember getting a strange feeling in my stomach. It wasn't a pleasant feeling, and I almost felt sick. It was as if I knew something bad was going to happen to this little girl, who was sitting on her bed, chattering away to me. I tried to ignore it and thought that perhaps it was because I was still feeling strange from my own operation. But the feeling didn't go away—I kept thinking that I was not going to see this girl ever again. After that, Susie spent more and more time lying in her bed. She slept a lot more, and there were always nurses coming to see her and check on her. She didn't show as much interest in playing with me or my toys.

On my last night at the hospital before I was to be discharged, I had a vivid dream about Susie on a playground. The sun was shining, it was a glorious day, and she was happy, full of energy and life. I saw myself standing, watching her on a swing, laughing, carefree, not in the least bit ill. Susie noticed me standing there, turned to me on one of her many swings back, smiled, and waved.

I remember waking up from this dream disoriented and unsure what to make of it. I looked over at Susie's bed, but the curtains were drawn. I never saw her again before I left.

My mother made me gather up all my things from the drawers—my clothes and my toys. I remembered the necklace that I so adored and the bag of plastic letters that I kept in the nightstand drawer. When I looked for it, the bag was there, but my necklace was gone. I looked in the bed and in the bag that I had just packed, but it wasn't there.

Suddenly, something made me turn around and look down on the floor by Susie's bed. I saw a multicolored strand of letters peeking out from under the curtains. I bent down to pick it up and saw the necklace with Susie's name in letters strung together with big hearts on either side of her name. I couldn't help but wonder what happened to Susie.

On the way out of the hospital, I asked a nurse if she could tell me about my roommate. My mother and the nurse exchanged a funny look.

"She's not here anymore, honey," the nurse replied. "She's gone home."

My mother was suddenly in a big hurry to leave. She interrupted the conversation, and I was disappointed that I never got a chance to ask the nurse what she meant. Deep inside of me, I had the feeling that Susie really never went home—not here, that is. Something told me that Susie had died and gone home to God.

Looking back, that is exactly what I saw in my dream. It was my first experience with a spirit visitation. And I suspect that the visit came just after Susie crossed over into spirit. Only later in my life and after a much longer list of spiritual experiences would I see that indeed that is what happens when people cross over. The experience with Susie was just the beginning.

I hung onto the necklace but never played with it again.

~ ~ ~

My grandfather Ivan died in 1973 after a brief battle with emphysema. He was a heavy smoker throughout his life, and his job as a miner contributed to his severe lung and health issues. Everybody in the family and many friends had tried hard to get him to quit smoking, but he was a stubborn and rigid man. I remember one night my mother and I went to my grandparents' home. I sat in a chair in a corner and watched my mother crying, desperately trying to reason with her father, whom she greatly adored. But Grandfather Ivan wouldn't listen to reason. His illness would land him in the hospital, hooked up to machines and encased in an oxygen tent. As I watched my mother and grandfather, I experienced that same feeling that I had when Susie spoke about her illness to me. It was a familiar, yet unsettling feeling, like I already knew something was going happen.

Later, my mother took me several times to visit my grandfather, sneaking me quietly into the hospital. In those days, there were restrictions on children being visitors, but I was glad I was allowed to go. I remember seeing my grandfather in his oxygen tent, with one armhole through which he could poke his arm to reach for something to drink on the side tray attached to the bed.

One day when we were visiting, my mother left me alone for a few minutes while she went off to find a nurse. Grandpa Ivan turned to me, his face slightly distorted through the plastic of the tent, and gently pushed his arm through the hole. He reached over and patted my face. I was crying. Inside, I knew that he was going to die. I didn't know how to express it in words, but instinct told me that this would be the last time I would see him.

His hand, though weak, tried to dry my tears. I could see and hear him mouthing the words, "Don't cry, Olena. I'm okay. Don't worry about me. I'll be fine. Take care of your mother."

Although I didn't comprehend what I, as a young girl, could do to take care of my mother, in hindsight he was obviously accepting the end of his mortality and welcoming his transition beyond this earthly life.

Days, maybe weeks later, Grandpa Ivan died. It was early in the morning. My mother woke me from my sound sleep. She came into my room crying. Her eyes were red and swollen. She put her arms around me and said, "Grandpa's gone, honey."

What was a child to do? I hugged her tightly, but I didn't have enough vocabulary to really know what to say. All I know is that the last time I cried was when I saw my grandfather in the hospital. I never cried for my grandfather after that. It was like deep down I had accepted that he was no longer with us.

Grandpa Ivan's funeral was crowded with many people from the Ukrainian community. I remember sitting at the back of the funeral home with my mother, surrounded by family and friends. She was distraught. Her father meant the world to her. I didn't understand why she was crying so much. For some reason, I found myself trying to console her.

"Mama," I said, as I placed my hand on hers, "Grandpa's not really here. It's okay, it's only his body up there," I stammered, referring to the casket. "Don't cry. Grandpa's fine."

"You don't know what you're talking about," my mother snapped at me, through her own tears and grieving.

I shut my mouth. I wanted desperately to explain to her that all of this wasn't real; that my grandfather's spirit was still here, and his body was just an empty shell. I could feel his presence everywhere that day. At that age though, I couldn't understand the concept of grieving over the physical body and couldn't comprehend the need for closure. I just wanted to reassure her he truly was alive, but we just couldn't see him.

That was the last time I mentioned anything about my grandfather to my mother. My grandfather had two funerals—one in the town where he lived and the second in the town where his body was finally buried, a five-hour drive from our home.

Finally, at the burial site, the very last ritual was over. It had been an extremely long and busy week. As with many burials, a headstone wasn't immediately put in place. Instead, a large wooden cross temporarily marked my grandfather's grave. I remember staring at the cross, almost mesmerized, like there was something pulling me toward it.

The priest said the final words, and every mourner dispersed, except me. I just couldn't walk away. There was something demanding my attention.

My eyes focused on a warm glowing light that appeared to me near the cross where a moment before there had been a crowd of people. I turned around quickly to see if anyone else saw this, but nobody was paying attention. They all had their backs to me and were walking away. My attention turned back to the light that I was seeing through a gray, rainy afternoon. I had no fear, but I was transfixed by it. The light took on a soft hazy shape. There was my Grandpa Ivan, standing in front of me.

As I watched him, my feet rooted to the ground. I could hear his words in my head: "I'm okay. Tell your mother I'm fine. Take care of her."

The light disappeared as quickly as it had come. I don't know what possessed me to do it, but I walked over to the cross and kissed it good-bye. Even though I knew he was there, and I had seen his spirit, it was as if I were saying good-bye to him.

I turned around and started running after the group of people, who by this time had quite a head start down the cemetery hill. It was November. The weather was cold and rainy, and I was scared that I would get lost, not knowing how to find my way back to the car. But I had made my closure.

After my grandfather's appearance, I felt peaceful and happy. I knew he was around me. But I also knew that what I had experienced was not typical. Since my mother didn't believe anything I said, I chose not to share that moment with her or with anyone else.

Psychic Awareness

The house that I grew up in was near the end of a very lengthy street which ran parallel to the Canadian Pacific Railway route. On the opposite end ran the Canadian National Railway tracks. My grandmother's house was somewhere in the middle of that street. The block was ethnically diverse, and there were at least half a dozen families around my house that had children close to my age. Most of the families were of European descent—Italian, Polish, German, Serbian, Yugoslavian, and many Ukrainians.

After my parents' separation, life for me became relatively sheltered and flat. I was never an extroverted child. I was the extremely shy, freckle-faced, knobby kneed, and very awkward kid, with glasses and braces. I found it difficult to approach people, especially children. Even though there were a lot of children surrounding my house, no one ever really got together and played. And there was almost no cross-cultural connection and play. Very few of us went to the same school, so the social aspect and common ground were limited. Everyone kept to their own yards. From my vantage point on the front lawn, I would often look at these children, riding their bicycles or playing hide and seek, and wish I could be less shy. For the most part, I kept to myself and became my own entertainer—and a creative, psychic one at that.

Instead of doing the usual kid things like riding bikes, throwing balls, or even fighting like many children do, I retreated into my own world, one that involved exercising and strengthening my psychic muscles. At the time, my reading was heavily focused on mysteries, especially Nancy Drew and the Hardy Boys stories.

I loved to play detective, and I enjoyed how these characters used their hunches and vibes to solve mysteries.

As I mentioned, our house was near the end of a long street. There was little traffic. Most of the activity occurred when the train that rumbled by our house several times per day. I started to become the psychic sleuth. My intuitive world started expanding, mostly by tuning into what was going on in and around my home. I would often hear my mother comment about the weather as she was hanging clothes on our clothesline—comments like, "It smells like rain," or, "It feels like snow tomorrow." I wondered how she knew that, because she was correct most of the time. Maybe she was psychic, too!

I would play intuitive games: tuning into the air outside and forecasting the night before what the weather would be like the next day; guessing when the next car would turn the corner on our street; predicting the exact time that the train would go through and how many box cars were attached to the train; and so on.

I included the animal realm in my intuitive games and spent countless hours staring at the ant hills, trying to see how long it took for the ants to climb out of the sand barrier that I had created as a challenge for them. As I lay on the grass staring at the sky, I wondered what winged creature would fly by my face next or what color it would be. Every spring I got into the habit of knowing how many baby birds would be born in the birdhouse above our garage.

Eventually, I graduated myself from being the kindergarten psychic and exchanged the tuning in to objects and animals for tuning in to people. I discovered that I had a knack for honing in on what their feelings were. Moreover, I could feel their emotions and see the disparity between what they felt and their spoken words. One of the discerning qualities of Indigos is the natural ability to be a lie detector. I could tell when people weren't telling the truth—like the time when my brother didn't came home after staying late at the university, working in the science lab.

My brother, eighteen at the time, was a science and biochemistry major, and much of his educational components involved experiments—lab rats, blood and tissue samples, and various creatures dissected and put on slides for analysis. He kept late hours. He would be home for dinner, and then drive back to the university lab throughout the week and weekend. He was still living at home while finishing his final years at college.

Because of the late hours that he spent away from home, my mother enforced a policy that he had to telephone at least once in the evening to make sure he was all right, *and* he had to be home before midnight. One night, he didn't do either. My mother was awake half the night, worried out of her mind. From my perspective, she was always protective of her first-born. The phone call finally came—at four in the morning.

I remember waking up to the jangling of the telephone, which scared me out of a sound sleep. I eavesdropped on the one-sided conversation. It was my brother, phoning to let my mother know that he had fallen asleep at the lab, and that he would be home in the morning. I didn't believe it—something just didn't feel right. For one thing, before my brother had left the house, I had watched him pay special attention to his appearance—too much attention in my opinion. I observed the clues—clean shirt, extra hair care, and fresh breath; all the little things that point to someone who was getting ready for a date.

I knew he wasn't telling the truth. I also intuited that he wasn't calling from the lab.

How could he lie like that? I thought. *And could my mother not know that he was not telling the truth? After all, wasn't the adult supposed to see through these things?*

My mother, however, bought the story, and actually felt sorry for him. I've often wondered how he got away with that one. When my brother got home in the morning, I practically pounced on him. He looked at me with disbelief, wondering what this little kid, his little sister, was doing.

"So where were you really?" I asked.

"I was at the lab, just like I said," Peter replied, visibly annoyed.

"No you weren't," I snapped back, with everything a little girl could muster. "I know you weren't there. So who were you with?"

"How would you know, and why would you care anyway?" he said, as he waved me away and stalked off.

But I did know. I didn't know quite how I knew, but I did. When I was around people, thoughts would just come into my head, sometimes feelings. I noticed that the more it happened, the more these thoughts would be accompanied by pictures of what was actually occurring. Much like all the music that I spent so long memorizing for a performance, pockets of information, words, or phrases would suddenly appear in my visual field. Later, I would learn that that was my mind's eye, sometimes called the third eye or chakra, open and at work. The thing was, I couldn't prove to someone what I knew; I just simply knew that I was right.

When I got older, my abilities expanded. I discovered that I could not only receive information in my mind and feel it in my body, but I could actually see into people's bodies. No, not in the X-ray vision sense, but I was able to tune in to a person's physical, mental, or emotional state.

That dramatic discovery of seeing the state of a person's health came with one of my elementary school teachers, Mrs. Molito. She was a petite, dark-haired Italian woman who exuded warmth and compassion. Next to my kindergarten teacher, Mrs. Molito was my favorite. She was gentle, motherly, and really cared about her students. They say that a teacher with a great personality and a love for teaching can really make a difference in a student's life. Mrs. Molito was that person, and I knew when I met her at the beginning of the school year that she was special.

I was especially drawn to her speech and her handwriting. Her writing on the chalkboard was exceptional—carefully and thoughtfully produced. I found myself admiring her writing and prided myself on learning how to copy it. As the saying goes, "Imitation is the sincerest form of flattery." It was through the handwriting that I aspired to be like Mrs. Molito.

In those days, learning the art of good penmanship was important. So much so, that the school awarded a prize for the students in each of the upper grades with the best penmanship. I practiced long and hard, even though I didn't really understand what it was that I was striving for. I figured that if I thought my writing looked great, then to me it was perfect. I struggled to understand how someone else could judge what perfect handwriting really was. *If I didn't have perfect penmanship, was that bad?*

This bothered me so much that I wanted to discuss how I felt about doing these little competitions with Mrs. Molito. She always encouraged her students to freely speak with her if something was on their minds. She spoke her mind as well, but in a way that was respectful and honorable. I felt good when I was around her.

One day after school, when the final bell rang, I lingered as the rest of the kids in the class stormed out, laughing and yelling. I wanted to talk to Mrs. Molito. I confess I also had an ulterior motive. The bullies I was contending with on a semiregular basis were still out in full force, and the more I lagged behind, the better the chance that they wouldn't be around when I got outside and started home.

That day had been a long one. Mrs. Molito had been away for several weeks on and off and had just returned. The vice principal of the school had substituted, and I was happy to have Mrs. Molito back.

As I walked to her desk at the front of the class, Mrs. Molito was cleaning the chalkboard. She looked tired. Her face, although a nice shade of olive that complimented her dark wavy hair, looked like she had something on her mind. As I drank in the sight of her, it occurred to me that she also looked thinner than the last time I had seen her. She handed me another eraser and asked me to help her out. I couldn't help wondering what was on her mind, and why she looked so tired, like she was dragging her body around.

"What is it that you wanted to talk to me about, Olena?" Mrs. Molito asked. My frustrations about the penmanship competition and my opinions on the stupidity of the whole thing poured out of me.

Patiently, she listened. "Olena, you can only do your best, and you are the only one that will know what that is. Don't ever strive to copy someone else," she said, almost as if she knew of my attempts to imitate her. "There just isn't enough time in your life to do that. You know, Olena, life is short, and spending time trying to be perfect isn't what really matters in life."

I watched Mrs. Molito's face carefully, and I listened to what seemed to be the enormity of that statement. As she spoke, I suddenly had this wave of images that flooded my mind, almost knocking me off my feet—they were so out of the blue and seemed to come from nowhere. I saw her lying in a hospital bed, surrounded my machines, her body hidden under the blankets. I tried to chase the pictures away, but they kept coming, rapidly and furiously. The more I tried to ignore what was flashing through my mind, the more they came.

While still looking like I was paying attention to what my teacher was telling me, my brain tried to grasp what I was seeing. Then I had another image. I "saw" the inside of her body. It appeared to me as if someone had opened an anatomy textbook, and I was viewing it. The picture I got was that her body looked like it was totally congested inside. Her organs were like gray shadows, and by my amateur description, her blood was sick. At least that's how it felt to me—total lack of energy. It became obvious to me that my favorite teacher was very ill.

I started to feel nauseous and couldn't figure out where that was coming from. I knew, though, that it had something to do with what I was seeing. The feeling that accompanied my vision, to my chagrin, was one that I was familiar with— the one where I knew that this person was dying and wouldn't be alive for too much longer.

I left her class that day trying to understand what I had just witnessed. After that, I looked at Mrs. Molito with different eyes. My whole being felt sad every time I looked at her, because I knew deep down that it was only a matter of time before something happened. I had been down that road before. I knew all too well the feeling of sensing when someone was ill and getting ready to cross over. All I could do was brace myself and wait.

I didn't have to wait too long. Mrs. Molito continued to be sporadically absent from the class. Eventually we were told that our substitute teacher would take over until the end of the school year. That news felt like a pit in my stomach. Within several months, my knowing proved real. As was routine for me, I was at home for lunchtime. When I returned to school after lunch, my class was buzzing with news. It seems I had missed an announcement by our principal that Mrs. Molito had died.

My heart sank. I didn't know how to behave or what to say. I just knew that I felt sad. But at the same time, I knew I had a secret that I couldn't share with others. I had known about her illness, and I knew she was not going to live through it. But I had enough smarts to know that I couldn't mention it to anyone. A part of me felt guilty and ashamed for knowing all of this, because I didn't know why I had these abilities or what to do with them.

At the funeral, I found out about Mrs. Molito's illness. She had had cancer, and her many absences from the class were due to her chemotherapy treatments, which resulted in her feeling sick and weak most of the time. It was only much later that I connected that information with how I experienced my intuition. The physical feeling of nausea must have been my way of picking up on her feelings and what her body was going through. The information about Mrs. Molito's cancer was a validation that what I saw was indeed real and correct. What I still didn't get, though, was why other people didn't experience what I did.

Angels on My Shoulder

I started racking up more of these spontaneous psychic experiences very quickly over a short period of time. The problem was that I still didn't understand how I knew what I knew or what I was supposed to do with everything that I discovered.

What I was aware of, though, was that in conjunction with the pictures that arrived in my mind and the feelings that I felt, I also heard messages in my head. It didn't happen often, but occasionally when a feeling about something came on, I could hear music in my head—not real music, but voices that were speaking in a musical way. I knew that it wasn't my own voice, and I knew that I couldn't have been making it up, first of all because it washed over me so quickly, and second, the musical tones were unlike anything that could be reproduced on this earth. I attempted to do that on many occasions on the piano. I also tried to sing the tones that I heard in my head, but to no avail, which was astounding, considering I had perfect pitch. I became convinced that this was beyond human experience.

The discovery of my enhanced auditory abilities intrigued me. I wanted more. It was clear that the knowledge I had didn't just come out of thin air, although it certainly seemed that away. It had to have come from somewhere. I decided that it wasn't enough for me to just sporadically hear, feel, or see things; I wanted to be able to talk to whomever it was that was responsible. Up to about age eight, I had not connected those dots. It had never occurred to me that I could consciously communicate with whatever was in the invisible realm that I had tapped into.

I recalled as a child having "invisible" friends that hung around, but it always seemed so one-sided. I took it for granted that they were there during stressful times in school or at home, and on occasion I poured out my heart to them. But I never thought to take an active role and have a dialogue—to ask questions and stop to listen for answers. By the time I was older, I couldn't even see the flashes of light or the angel beings anymore. Any vibes or information that I received within me just came; I never consciously asked for any of it. So I wondered, *where did all the angels go?*

I added conversation to the mix of my self-taught psychic development classes. As a child, if someone caught me seemingly talking to myself, no one would have thought anything of it. After all, invisible friends in a child's life are pretty common. Most people don't take it seriously. They view it as something not entirely real or a phase that eventually will be outgrown. As I got older, I recognized that talking to myself out loud, especially in a place that wasn't private, would be looked on as mighty strange. So I did the smart thing and kept it to myself.

But secretly I enjoyed using my newly discovered abilities. I especially enjoyed testing myself and those invisible beings around me. The more I started asking, the more I started hearing and receiving answers. Question after question would pour out of my mind.

What should I eat for breakfast today? Which road should I take home from school (to avoid the bullies)? *What should I wear today? Is my mother in a good mood or bad mood? Should I be careful about what I say to her if she's in a bad mood? Who is on the other end of the phone? Will my auntie's dog be at my house when I get home from school?*

Every time I asked something, answers came. They came as a soft whisper in my mind, sometimes like tinkling musical notes and sometimes like a booming chorus of voices. I got in the habit of checking in with my invisible helpers daily. It helped me survive many of the adversities in my life.

I almost keeled over the day I heard the voice of what I know now as my guardian angel. Until that point, I accepted everything for what it was—nameless, faceless, body-less beings that simply hung around me and were my 24/7 bodyguards, guardians, counselors, and advisers. I finally got up the courage one day to ask for a name. The human brain got the better of me and wanted something to grab on to. It seemed more fun that way and more real to talk to something or someone if it had a name.

My new bedroom was in an attic on the top floor of my grandmother's house. It was quiet and fairly private. If there was any talking out loud, I could do it easily either hiding under the blankets or retreating further into the cozy attic.

At night, I would focus on the black space, staring into nothingness and unburdening myself of everything that happened in my day and talking about how I felt. I could feel my helper's presence around me, just like a mother tucking her child into bed, making me feel safe and nurtured.

The energy would often feel like a female, so one night I decided that I was ready to know who this was. "Who are you?" I whispered. "What is your name?"

Silence. I sat up in the still darkness, blanket tucked around me, the house quiet, and all lights out. It was just me and my space. More silence.

After what seemed like an eternity, I wasn't getting anything, so I flopped back down onto my pillow, exasperated. I just knew something was around me, *so what was the problem?* I wondered.

But just as my eyes were getting heavy, and I was starting to drift off into sleep, I heard a voice in my head in a way that I had never heard before. It was a soft voice, not musical as I had been used to, but a solid, confident, yet very loving voice. And it said, "I am Mary. I love you very much."

Wow, I thought, *Mary.* Mary was my grandmother's name. Mary was my middle name, too. I was surrounded by people named Mary. At first I thought I was making it up. It was too close to home. But the curious tester part of me kept right on going. I was curious and needed further proof that this was real. *I want to see you,* I cried in my head. *If this is real, please show me what you look like,* I asked.

And just like my experience with the hand of God and the experience at my grandfather's funeral, in the blackness of the ceiling above, I began to see a haze of light. This time, though, it didn't move like my previous experiences. It unfolded like a flower opening its petals. The light got brighter, and out of it I could see the shape of a woman. Her hair shone, and a baby blue cloak surrounded her. I could tell that she had dark yet kind eyes. Her energy was so loving and warm. I felt my heart fill with love and joy.

Mary looked almost like the Mother Mary icon that I had grown up seeing on the wall. She *was* real! I couldn't believe it. It wasn't wishful thinking after all! I jumped for joy inside. And in my heart of hearts I made the ultimate confession to her.

I told Mary I wanted her to be my mother. I never got an answer to that. Mary just smiled at me, and I felt waves of love surround my heart. Eventually I faded off into sleep, knowing within myself that for the first time I felt protected and loved, and nothing could ever hurt me. I had Mary to turn to for comfort.

I started to have constant conversations with Mary. Although I didn't see her all the time, I knew she was there. I was acutely aware of her, especially during times of stress in my life—walking to and from school with bullies making my walk difficult, or when my mother was secretly drinking or on medication and decided to take her upsets out on me. It was nice to know that I had someone to turn, someone to have faith in, someone to trust—and that was Mary.

One warm summer night, as my mother was moving our belongings to my grandmother's house, my faith was tested, and the protection surrounding me became clear. My grandfather Ivan had long since passed away, and my grandmother was alone in the house. I had had no desire to go into my grandparents' home since my grandfather died, out of fear that I might see him again physically. Getting older had opened the door to fear. As a child, I didn't feel afraid when I saw spirits, but in the psychic "off hours," I didn't like surprises. More fears and doubts started to creep into my mind as I got older and faith lessened. I had visions of walking into a room, and my grandfather would be there, or I'd turn a corner, and he'd jump out. I became doubtful, not of whether spirits existed (that I was sure of), but of how to deal with them and their unexpected visitations.

By this time, I knew that I would be living with my grandmother, despite any protests. I reasoned that if my grandfather was around, then I needed to take charge of the situation.

Just like my conversations with Mary, I started to have a one-way conversation with my grandfather. As if he were physically standing in front of me, I told him that it is was okay if he was there, but I asked that if he planned to show himself to me, to please do it gently. It was bad enough that the rest of my waking life with live human beings was like walking on eggshells. I didn't need the dead surprising me on top of that. Since I didn't have anyone to talk to about this, I stayed in that fear place for a very long time.

Years later when I started refining my abilities as a medium, I realized that the fears I felt while in the house were other people's emotions and fears and had nothing to do with spirits or the spirit realm. In short, I learned that being in the living world was scary—the spirit world was anything but.

During the transition between homes, we would stay partially at my grandmother's house and partially at our old home while my mother figured out what possessions were to be sold, packed away, or moved. On one of the nights that we were staying at my old home, my mother was busy packing and sorting. We were having a yard sale the next day, so she was embroiled in a flurry of activity. My grandmother was away for the week; several times a year she would take a trip to Southern Ontario with one of my uncles to visit relatives and friends and my grandfather, at the cemetery. Because the trip was at least five hours by car, my grandmother always turned the journey into a brief holiday. And during the times that she was away, my mother would either housesit or keep an eye on the house during her absence.

That evening my mother was absorbed in her packing. My grandmother was away, so my mother decided that I should run up the hill to the house and check on it. That meant that I had to go into the house and walk around to make sure no one had broken in. She was quite fastidious about making sure that all doors and windows were checked and all electrical appliances were unplugged. It was not something that I really wanted to do. However, the thought of being away from my mother for at least forty-five minutes sounded quite appealing.

It was early evening with dusk settling in when my mother commanded me to go to my grandmother's house. The dark and I were friends while I was safe under my blankets in bed, but I wasn't comfortable walking outside in the dark by myself. In fact, it was downright scary.

To my knowledge, not a single crime occurred the whole time that I resided on our street. I would often run or bike my way up our hilly street and visit my grandmother during the daytime by myself and think nothing of it. But this was another thing altogether. With my fear of invisible spirits popping out at me when I was least prepared, I had no desire to go through with this task.

But I grudgingly went, under strict instructions by my mother to walk under the street lamps. That way, if anything happened, I could run up someone's driveway to the nearest house. Seeing as I had no intention of even going into the house once I got there, I had to figure out a way of proving to my mother that I had been dutiful and completed a thorough check.

When I got there, the house was pitch black—no lights were on inside or out. My fear rose right into my mouth. I could practically taste it. There was no way I was going into that house, especially since the way in was to walk around the side of the house, go through a creaky little green gate, and walk up the back steps— all invisible from the street. If a bogeyman was lurking in the back, I would be snatched, never to be heard from again—and no one would see it happen.

So, I did what my smarts told me do. In hindsight, maybe it was the invisible helpers who were always with me and guided me along. I went around the side of the house up to the gate, opened it, and never went through it. I just stood there for a while, praying to God to help me get through this, and of course giving myself enough time to convince my mother that I had done my job. Satisfied, I decided enough was enough, and I left.

It was dark by now, and with my mother's lingering instructions ringing in my ears, I started running down the street and down the hill. The street was rather lengthy, running parallel to the train tracks, and between my house and my grandmother's was a small perpendicular connector street, like a T. If you followed it, you'd reach the next parallel block of houses. I always hated that tiny little intersection, and the dark amplified it. Every time I went by that little street, I had a habit of looking down it to make sure a car wasn't approaching or someone wasn't walking down it. After I managed to walk by that intersection, I knew the rest of the way down the hill would be simple, as every house was in plain view.

Just as I got to the intersection, my pace picked up. I felt something like a chill go up my spine. It didn't feel good, and something inside of me urged me to run faster. The second house from the corner of the intersection was a bright yellow house. I was familiar with the family who lived there. They had several older daughters, all of whom were friendly and waved or spoke to us when my mother and I walked by. I was almost at the yellow house when something made me turn and look down the intersection.

Under a street lamp, about halfway down the street, I saw the outline of a man. It looked like a very tall man. He was just standing there, not moving, but he was definitely looking in my direction. I had no idea who he was or why he was there, but I knew that it was bad. And my psychic radar rose higher than it ever had been before. I knew that person had bad intentions. I still had ten minutes to go though before I could get to my house, even at a very fast run.

A voice in my head boomed, "Olena, go into the house, now!"

I listened.

I was right in front the yellow house. Like a Christmas tree, all the lights were on, and I could feel a huge force steering me from behind. It made me run up that driveway. I ran up and knocked on the door.

Thankfully, the lady who lived there answered the door and recognized me as living down the street. I explained to her that there was a man standing down the street, and that I was scared to walk the rest of the way by myself.

"Would someone be willing to take me home?" I stammered.

There truly were angels around me that night. I knew deep inside of me that if I had continued by myself and ignored the messages and feelings that I was being given, I may have been harmed or even killed. Two of the daughters in that house walked me home.

As we were going down the hill, I felt that chill up my back again. Something made me turn around and look behind me. There was the man, standing under the street lamp at the corner of the street, just where I had been a mere ten minutes earlier. I hadn't imagined it after all. The whole thing felt creepy. Until I left home and moved away from that city, I never walked the streets alone in the dark again.

Although I was commended for being brave and doing the right thing by my earth angels who walked me home, my mother didn't really make any fuss about it. I do not have any recollection of her hugging me, asking me if I was all right, or acknowledging my terrified feelings. She was very matter of fact with me when I got through the door and left her listening to the two lovely girls recounting what had happened. I was instructed to go take a bath and get ready for bed. I was disappointed in her behavior and reaction. I thought my being safe would be high on her list of parent priorities, but for some reason, it wasn't. My trust in my mother plummeted in those few minutes.

Internally, I vowed never to do what my mother did. I was determined at a young age that, should I ever be a mother, I would never take my children for granted.

That night was an eye-opener. I learned other major lessons that day as well. There was no doubt in my mind that the voices inside my mind and my feelings were real, that angels and guides truly existed, that my trust and faith in the invisible won hands down over the visible, *and* that it was important that I listen constantly and never doubt what I heard, saw, or felt.

I Just Want to Be Normal

CHAPTER FIVE

Be who you are and say what you feel, because those who mind don't matter and those who matter don't mind.[5]

—Dr. Seuss
American author and illustrator

The fate of my teenage years was determined not by me, but by my mother, who was overseer of my education. I was not included in decisions that were made about my care and well-being or the direction of my life, education, or otherwise. Allowing children the power of free choice was just not in my mother's consciousness, and I suspect not very pervasive in the society in which I lived.

On the day of my graduation from elementary school, my mother and I were walking home from the end of year ceremonies. Two nuns were walking in the opposite direction, and we recognized one of them as my music teacher, Sister Victoria. The other nun was introduced as Sister Bonnie from the same religious order. She lived in the "Sister House" along with Sister Victoria. My mother stopped and conversed with the two sisters, mentioning that I had just graduated eighth grade and was entering high school. Until then, I hadn't given it much thought. I had no clue what the next steps were for my life. Imagine my surprise when my mother announced that she had enrolled me in the Catholic all-girls school, the school that housed the music school where I went for piano lessons every week! Without skipping a beat and with great interest, Sister Bonnie proclaimed that she would teach one of my ninth-grade classes.

I groaned silently. When the impact of that news settled in, I started to get angry, but I had to force my feelings inward. My mother's treatment of me had become so bad, that I had learned to keep quiet and not trigger any more emotions than necessary. If I opened my mouth and offered my opinion, I got hit, slapped, or yelled at. She didn't care which part of my body she hit. My mother didn't believe children should have opinions. Her motto was that children should be seen and not heard. What she didn't know was that her precocious twelve-year-old daughter was about to start bucking the rules and discover her own voice.

I could not believe that I wasn't asked for my thoughts on which high school I wanted to attend. There was more than one school in the district where I lived, and school buses were available to take you to school. I had watched other kids ride the bus in elementary school but never had the opportunity to be on one myself. I lived too close to the elementary school to qualify for the bus, but with the high school further way, the bus suddenly became feasible. I had always wanted to ride a school bus and going to a high school of my choosing would have also given me that opportunity to experience it.

So in September of 1980, I entered Marymount, a Christian high school run by the Sisters of Saint Joseph, focusing on a Roman Catholic education. The irony was that I wasn't the least bit religious, even though my family and culture was immersed in it. I wasn't Roman Catholic and knew nothing about that variation of the Christian faith. My mother had enrolled me in the high school using my now-deceased grandmother's Catholic status as proof that someone in the family was Catholic, a prerequisite for acceptance into this school. My grandmother had converted to the Greek Orthodox faith when she married my grandfather, but she still had her Catholic baptismal certification.

My mother's view of the male population was pretty much negative, especially after the separation from my father. She believed that if I associated with boys, I would be distracted from my education; surrounded by liars, thieves, and troublemakers; and barefoot and pregnant by the time I was eighteen. Sending me to an all-girls school instead of the local coed high school would protect me from the big, bad boys. Additionally, she condoned corporal punishment and the belief that children should be disciplined as needed. Having her daughter surrounded by nuns wielding the power of punishment was music to her ears. To me it felt like a prison.

So I showed up on the first day school wearing the school uniform in all its glorious colors—dull gray and dark blue. The precise specifications of the clothes shocked me: A-line skirt of a specific length, white blouse with starched collar, cardigan sweater with the school crest, knee socks that you had to keep pulled up, and straight gray pants in the winter. The school's theory that uniforms removed any sense of competition, fads, and cliques, and promoted, pardon the pun, a sense of uniformity through all the girls.

A myriad of strict rules existed—no makeup, no perfume, no fancy hair, no jewelry unless it was a cross, no high heels, no foul language, no gum chewing. The list seemed endless. Any student caught breaking any of these rules would be reprimanded and could be suspended if the rules were continuously challenged. Not one to conform to rules, I wondered how I would survive the next five years in the large brick building on the hill. I lost my faith in everything and began wishing that I were dead, rather than being subjected to all this.

Because Marymount was based on the Roman Catholic faith, one of the mandatory requirements was that the students' lives clearly revolve around God and the saints. We were to confess sins regularly, know the Hail Mary in our sleep, and attend Mass. Of course, that assumed every person attending the school was Catholic and understood what that entailed. Since I was neither Roman nor Catholic, I had no clue what it all meant and had no familiarity with any Catholic practices. Other than Mother Mary, my invisible protector, and the twelve apostles, my knowledge about many of the Catholic saints was scanty at best! Once a week all the students would troop into the school gymnasium where a Catholic Mass was celebrated. Thankfully enough, I had grown up around church rituals and was at least familiar with long church services and partaking of bread and wine.

Sister Gloria was the principal. She was a tall, serious, no-nonsense woman, who believed that all girls needed to be well disciplined in the words of our Lord and Savior Jesus Christ. She was the main overseer of the hourlong Mass. Each girl had know the Lord's Prayer by heart and must know how to take proper Communion, which included knowing what to say before and after the wine hit one's mouth—no arguments, no exceptions.

There was no chance to sit out Communion. You either had to be incapacitated or have the holiest of excuses to not partake of the body and blood of Jesus Christ. Since I was unfamiliar with the practices, I started to listen hard and pay attention to what the girls in front of me in the line were doing and saying.

The problem was I felt like a fake. I couldn't believe that I had to go through all this pretending that I truly believed that through that physical act I was allowing God and Jesus Christ into my life. I mean, the wine wasn't really Jesus' blood, and it felt funny to eat Jesus' body that tasted like cardboard. I had experienced the hand of God in my sleep, and Jesus and Mary had been part of my life without any physical props.

I felt like I was immersed in a grand production. Falling into line like an obedient little fake Catholic girl was downright wrong. So wrong that I started breaking the rules and speaking out. I discovered how catalytic my voice really was through Sister Clara, my English teacher.

Not one class day ever started without the reciting of the Lord's Prayer. Every morning, the announcement and bell would blare, signaling everyone to get out of their desks, face the wall with Jesus and Mother Mary icons adorning it, and say the prayer God gave us in unison.

I felt so awkward stating words that meant nothing to me. I didn't see the purpose of doing something the same way, in the same routine, day after day. Why should I have to verbalize words repeatedly to affirm God's existence for myself? Don't get me wrong; I had nothing against praying. It just didn't feel right for me to use words that were extremely limiting. Repeating them wouldn't bring me any closer to God. I fully embrace prayer, but I see it as a conscious dialogue with God, instead of a ritual where words are mouthed without being aware of *why* they are being used.

After my own experiences with challenging the religion that I grew up with, I had a hard time getting into the religious game—a game that just didn't fit me. Saying my prayers in my own way was more my style. Anything along the lines of, "Dear God, please help me have a great day today," or "Please help me ace my French test today," would have been my preference.

One day I found myself laughing about exactly that with the girl sitting behind me in Sister Clara's class. We were taking a test on Shakespeare that day. Everyone had to memorize a monologue from *Hamlet* and be prepared to explain it to the class. I was not totally prepared—I had the monologue memorized, but the comprehension of the archaic language eluded me.

Because I didn't understand it, I was having a problem retaining the monologue and became mentally bored. The more bored I became, the more rebellious I behaved. Like my musical training, I had learned that I could rely on retrieving the information from inside of me, visually seeing it in my head when push came to shove. If that failed, I would go internally and praying to God to help me remember.

So on that day, I was prepared not to do well on this exam. I came to school tired and had no energy to get through my classes. All the girls were talking excitedly, perhaps nervously, among themselves, waiting for Sister Clara to arrive.

Upon entering high school, I dropped some of my shyness and developed the habit of turning to the person sitting behind me in the row and talking to them, no matter what class I was in. That day, Laurie was behind me.

"So, did you memorize it?" I turned around and asked Laurie, referring to the exam.

"No, not everything," she said with a half smile. "I'm not sure how I'm going to do. Maybe Sister Clara won't call on everybody today. I mean there's not enough time in the class for her to go through everybody. So just pray that she won't call our names."

I whooped for joy inside at the thought of asking God not to have Sister Clara call my name. It was like Laurie could read my mind.

"Hey," I said, "c'mon let's do it together!"

I figured the power of two was stronger than the power of one, and I truly believed that if I put out the intention that I wouldn't be singled out. It would happen just the way I visualized it. After all, I had experienced many successes with this practice through my music performances, so why not use it for everything else?

"Dear God…" I started chanting formally, pretending to sound like Sister Clara. I spoke loudly enough for the kids in the neighboring seats to turn around. "Puhleeeze let Sister Clara ask someone else to get up and speak in front of the class today, and let it not be meeeeeee!" I droned on, oblivious that Sister Clara had walked into the class.

A hush descended. My final words hung in the air. Everyone had heard them, including Sister Clara. Moreover, I wasn't sitting in my seat facing the blackboard. That was a general rule in our class, and I had broken it. Sister Clara, a much older and very stern nun, walked by my desk, staring at me angrily. She was very strict and conservative in her views, especially on how children should behave and be disciplined. She didn't tolerate laughing and being joyful in her class. Being pious and solemn was more befitting for young Catholic ladies in her eyes.

Sister Clara pushed her horn-rimmed glasses up onto her nose and stopped in front of me, with her long black skirt swishing around her, tapping a very long ruler on the floor.

"Was there something you wanted to share with the class, young lady?" she demanded. "C'mon now, don't keep me waiting. We don't have all day you know."

"Well, Sister," I stammered, utterly terrified by now, "I was just asking God to help me with my exam today."

"You asked what of God? You can't ask God directly for something! Don't you lie to me young lady!" Sister Clara gurgled, her eyes starting to bulge. She looked like she was going to have a stroke or heart attack right then and there.

I sat there not knowing what I was supposed to say, but I suddenly had the feeling I knew how Jesus felt as he was being crucified for simply being who he was and what he knew.

"I'm not lying, Sister," I stammered courageously, "I talk to God all the time—no big deal."

That did it. Sister Clara didn't know what to make of my answer. Right then, I knew I had pushed her to the edge.

"Blasphemy! How dare you mock the Lord?" she cried as she lifted the ruler and whacked my hands, which were lying on the desk. "That'll teach you not to make fun of what's sacred here."

I fought back hot, stinging tears. I felt humiliated by being physically punished in front of the whole class for something that to me wasn't wrong. The rest of the class shrank into their seats. Nobody wanted to be next and did not dare saying anything to contradict the furious sister.

"Don't you ever let me catch you lying again, or I will send you to the principal's office, and you will be suspended from school." Sister Clara yelled at me, as she slapped my hands once more with the ruler. "I never want to hear you say that again. May God have mercy on you. Your penance is twelve Hail Marys, and—go to confession."

Whatever that means, I thought. Was I a sinner now that I talked to God? And what exactly did I have to confess? Obviously she thought I had done something wrong, and perhaps to her, God was too lofty for the ordinary folk to talk to. But my wave of fright lasted only but a few minutes. My inner defiance took over, and I sat out the rest of the class in silence. But my prayer was granted. I never got called on to do my monologue. Technically, I guess, I already had, though just in a way that I hadn't planned.

I realized that what I said had an effect. I wasn't sure what I was supposed to do with this realization just yet, but I recognized that I had the ability to voice what I believed to be true inside of me and see how deeply it could affect other people, even driving them to great anger.

My rebellious streak was only starting to kick in. So was my voice.

I Just Want to be Accepted

I had finally made some friends at this school. With the exception of the some of the teachers, the school was free of the male gender. However, that didn't mean that girls couldn't be wild and crazy. They were. As I entered my teen years with great awkwardness and trepidation, I found myself befriended by the people who displayed the most outward rebellion and took risks—exactly the opposite of the pious, straight-and-narrow students that were supposed to be the heart and soul of the high school.

Nicky was one of those people. I connected with her quickly at Marymount. She was a bit of a daredevil. We bonded over ninth grade typing class. At last, someone who was nice and wanted to talk to me and accepted me for whom I was! That was the year of prime-time hunk-filled television shows like *Magnum PI*, *CHiPs*, and *The Dukes of Hazzard*. Because the life I lived was extremely sheltered, television in my home was controlled and for the most part prohibited. Whenever I watched anything, it had to be mother-approved. Any TV viewing was considered a treat and usually coincided with my mother's better moods.

We received only two channels on a 1960s television set, so my ability to access programs was limited. But this was 1981, and typical girl conversations revolved around boys, often TV stars. We especially liked the tall, dark, and handsome ones, as well the "bad boy" varieties—the more "bad," the better. Even though I wasn't able to keep up with the weekly programming, Nicky would keep me up-to-date on the goings of each show. "Did I see that shirt Magnum wore that night?" she'd ask. Or, "Did I see how Luke Duke slid across the car in those jeans?" Over the noisy *clack clack* of the typewriters, each of us speed typing as quickly as possible within the sixty-second drills, I would get the lowdown on these exciting characters. And exciting they were to me. The more I heard, the more I desired to be free and live on the edge, like they did. What intrigued me the most were characters who always got into trouble, were even willing to break the law slightly while fighting for the underdog, and yet their great charm and wit somehow pulled them out of it.

One day walking from class, giggling about something secretly discussed over the noise of the typewriters, Nicky decided to dare me to do something out of the norm, on the edge. She always told me that I was too serious, too uptight, and that I needed to lighten up and have some fun. She was probably right. I didn't know how to have fun. I probably didn't even know what fun looked or felt like. But my brain was intrigued at the prospect of breaking rules and living a little on the edge, even with something that potentially might get me into a bit of trouble.

The dare, made up on the spot, was simple. We were in the girls' bathroom, and Nicky noticed that someone had left a pile of books and a calculator sitting on the window ledge. She dared me to take that calculator, pocket it, go into the bathroom, and put it back when I came out.

"Oh, I don't know," I said.

"C'mon," Nicky wheedled. "There's no one here. Someone obviously forgot it, and you'll have it back there in no time. No one will ever know. Go for it."

I hesitated. She was right. No one was there, and I would only be in the bathroom for a few minutes. I guessed that I could take a chance. I figured there wasn't any harm in something that no could see happening. So I did it. I pocketed the calculator, all the while with this loud, nagging voice inside my head, warning me, "Olena, don't. Put it back." I beat the voice back and chose to ignore it. The challenge of the dare and wanting Nicky to like me was far more of a lure than the doing the right thing.

I closed the door to the bathroom stall. Just then, the main restroom door opened. A bunch of girls came running in, one of whom I distinctly heard loudly proclaiming that she had forgotten her books. Seconds later the girl noticed that her calculator was missing. Frantically she looked around everywhere trying to find it. And there I was, caught in the restroom stall, knowing full well I had it on me.

I freaked out. I hadn't listened to my inner voice, and it had proved itself once again to be a great guidance system. I felt trapped and didn't know how to get out of it. Several scenarios ran through my head. I could have come out, admitted what I had done and why, apologized, and that might have been the end of it. Keeping the calculator on me would have been far worse. So I did the cowardly thing and went right down the middle. I left the calculator in the stall. After all, if I was going to get into trouble, there was no way I wanted to be caught with the evidence on me. I came out of the stall with the best poker face I could muster. When asked me if I had seen the calculator, I lied and said I hadn't.

It would have ended there had it not been for one of the girls deciding to go to the principal. My poker face must have been pretty lousy, because suddenly there were more people involved, and the situation got out of hand. Because Nicky and I were the only two students who had been in the bathroom, we were the most likely suspects. And I must have looked the guiltiest. It was a humiliating situation. Both of our lockers were searched from top to bottom by the vice principal. Of course, neither of us had the calculator, so it was never found. Neither of us ever revealed what really happened.

I was banned from visiting my locker at any time other than morning, lunch, and afternoon, and Nicky and I were not allowed to see or talk to each other anymore. I was suspended from school for one day. Of course, my mother got called in which made it far worse. She was angry and infuriated at my involvement in a potential crime, and, according to her, I was an embarrassment. I felt horrible about the situation. What I wasn't aware of was that I was already suffering from depression, with no one around to recognize what lay beneath it—anger.

Psychic Shut Down

I entered grade ten with a lot of ambivalence. The remaining high school years—four more to be exact (in Eastern Canada high school was five years long)—seemed to stretch ahead, as if they would never end. The classes that I had to take to fulfill the requirements were, in my mind, boring. Left-brain-oriented subjects, like physics and math, were not my strong suit.

It was difficult for me sit in class learning statistics or doing experiments. I could not see how they would be useful in the world outside of school unless your goal was to pursue these as a career. The only sciences that kept my attention were biology and chemistry. I loved to learn about evolution and how things operated anatomically. Dissecting frogs and other critters appealed to me. While some kids abhorred smelling formaldehyde and viewing internal organs, I discovered that I had a great disassociation from these practices. Much to my amazement, I had no qualms watching an operation like brain or heart surgery. I was fascinated with the way the human system operated, from the physical to the psyche. I'm sure that in a previous life, I was a physician or something similar. It is no surprise that later in life I had no difficulty poking needles into my patients' bodies during acupuncture sessions. Chemistry was just plain creative. Combining elements and creating something new appealed to me.

I also enjoyed creative writing, health, dramatic arts, and band. I could see myself potentially pursuing music, being a professional musician, traveling from city to city, and performing to large audiences. Wow, I thought, how wonderful! I already had years of training toward being a concert pianist, so this fantasy wasn't a big stretch.

The Beatles were like gods to me. They represented freedom—the freedom of being unrestricted, living true to your soul, playing music, traveling, writing, being creative, not being bound by others' expectations. I fantasized about that and believed it was possible in my future.

The problem was the dichotomy in which I lived. How could I deal with the struggle within me? I enjoyed learning about subjects that spoke to my heart, but I didn't see the point in some of the "core" courses that didn't speak to me whatsoever.

I balked at everything that someone else told me was important for me. I couldn't comprehend how anyone else could decide what was important in my life. Besides, why didn't I get to choose what courses appealed to me? The heart of my angst was the frustration and lack of freedom to choose. I thought that having a student's input into their own educational picture would be a positive thing.

While students may be inattentive due to lack of interest or poor presentation of the course material, I look back and wonder if the main reason for the inattentiveness is the lack of student involvement in their educational choices. If choice was a major component, then the personal appeal would naturally be there. Knowing that an Indigo is vehement about free choice and will resist anything that smacks of restriction of that freedom, these thoughts explained why I felt what I felt.

As a result of my vast boredom, I drifted through school. I went from being a great student, mentally quick, a fast learner, and basically a straight A achiever, to being a depressed, fatigued, uninterested, practically failing student, with no desire and no sense about the rest of her life. My spirit was at a low point, and I was ripe for stirring up more trouble.

Instead of doing homework, I would spend hours drawing patterns with my compass. Mandalas took the place of math; sleep took the place of mostly everything else. I attracted new school friends who seemed just as bored as I was. Lisa and Sheila became my new, non-cool friends. We discovered that we had a lot in common. We had divorced or separated parents, we defied rules and regulations, we had no sense of our own life direction, and we viewed high school as a prison.

One day Lisa introduced me to her secret habit—smoking cigarettes. Smoking, drinking, and using any kind of mood-altering substances were prohibited by the school and were also things that my mother had taught me were horrible sins. The irony was that my mother said one thing but demonstrated another through her abuse of prescription drugs and alcohol. Also, my father was a heavy smoker, as had been my grandfather. So I was bombarded with mixed messages about what was considered right and wrong. But what my parents did outweighed what they said. My father smoked, so I figured *why not?* My mother had a habitual practice of drinking and downing prescription drugs with caffeinated soft drinks.

Not wanting to appear different to my new friends, I went along with everything they proposed. We were settling down in physics class one day, when Lisa pulled out her book bag and gave me a peek inside. There was an open pack of cigarettes and several miniature bottles of alcohol, like the kind found in hotel room mini-bars.

"Where did you get that?" I asked.

"From my parents' liquor cabinet—they always have stuff that like lying around," Lisa proclaimed.

I was shocked when I saw them. First, I thought that was so bold of her to bring them into the school, knowing full well what school policy was. Even more, I wasn't sure how I should handle it. I didn't want to let on that I was feeling so uncomfortable. I wanted to be accepted. That meant that I would have to pretend I was very cool and nonchalant about the whole thing.

Lisa leaned over and whispered, "Let's meet at lunchtime behind the school."

I was torn between looking like this was no big deal and being aware that I'd be taking risks and defying authority. To me, being accepted meant that I was normal, just like everyone else. And I wanted so badly to be normal. I had had enough of being different. So, I opted for normalcy, or what seemed like it at the time.

Luckily, we didn't get caught. I never let on to Lisa that it was my first time trying to smoke a cigarette or slugging back a mouthful of alcohol. Outside of my mother's or father's habits, my family rarely drank alcohol. The only alcohol that I had been introduced to was at my church, where Communion was administered with real bread soaked in strong, sweet red wine. In the end, I realized that I didn't like how drinking made me feel. I must have had an extremely low tolerance, because shortly after the first swig, I felt horribly sick to my stomach and very lightheaded.

All through the rest of that day, I used all my willpower to make sure that I looked and walked normally. Externally, I looked put together. Internally, my brain and body were numb. *That* feeling I didn't like. The strange thing was that I enjoyed the taste of alcohol, especially wine, but the residual feeling was so profoundly negative, that I didn't pursue it further—not that I could've anyway, since I was underage and had no money to speak of.

Cigarettes were another matter. Lisa and I made it a habit to sneak off outside the school and take quick drags off the sticks that she would swipe from her home. Unlike alcohol, I didn't like the taste of cigarettes, but I did enjoy the way I felt. It would soothe my anxiety, and any feelings of angst, sadness, or anger would miraculously melt away. I never had to think when I was smoking a cigarette.

Unbeknownst to me, the habit was altering my mood, and my intuitive connections were slowly shutting down. But I didn't care. I just wanted to look normal. Although I never smoked openly, there were many times that I was afraid I would get caught. I was always aware of that possibility, so I took great care of making sure no one was around before I headed out to my private place, sitting on the grassy hill behind the school.

I don't know if it made me a cool kid or not, but I know that hanging out with Lisa and some of her friends made me feel normal. The occasional cigarette, not doing homework, and skipping an occasional class quickly bought me acceptance in these girls' eyes.

My intuitive abilities fell by the wayside. The more I moved into the world of Lisa and her friends, the more I didn't have to pay attention to the quiet voices and direction inside of me. By this time, my sixth sense, which used to surround me all the time, seemed to have dissipated and only came sporadically.

I even stopped consciously turning to God for the most part. I enlisted God's help only rarely, such as when I was having a bad day at school and was worried about my mother punishing me for bad grades, or when I was about to face yet another music competition and I prayed to God to help me win.

Now I had the approval of my new friends, but my self-esteem was at an all-time low. Anything invisible, such as my intuitive abilities, became low on my list.

My last-ditch attempt to escape my non-normalcy came through television. Though my television watching was restricted, there were some shows I could watch, such medical or legal dramas like *Perry Mason* or *Quincy, M.E.*, or comedy shows like *One Day at a Time* or *Bosom Buddies*. I was a strongly visual person, so much of my intuitive information would come through in that way, more so than other methods of reception. Images on screen would be a trigger for me. Television, in fact, became an addiction. It not only seemed to feed and stimulate my brain, but it activated my sensory perceptions. Sometimes I thought I was hallucinating, especially since I experienced a lot of daily fatigue and growing feelings of hopelessness.

But whenever I would watch a program, images beyond what I was seeing would sporadically pop into my mind. In the middle of a show or watching a news report, I would suddenly get information visually and through my feelings about a person I was watching. The images and feelings took on a common theme—mostly about illness and death. I'd see a face, some celebrity or well-known person, and get a flash in my mind that they were ill and battling a disease. If it was a chronic or life-threatening illness, the feeling inside of me would come on quite strongly. I noticed after a while that the clearer the visual and the stronger the feelings, the closer the timeline as to when the person I was seeing would no longer be alive.

As morbid as it may sound, I slowly realized that I could tell when a person was getting ready to die. Not specifically when, because that I believe is between the person and the creator, but simply that their life was drawing to a close. I intuitively knew it. What was worse, the end usually came within a short time of me "seeing" it. My visions always involved famous people—celebrities, actors, musicians, people in the public eye. John Belushi, Rock Hudson, and Elvis Presley were three of those people. I know what you're thinking. Yes—Elvis. That was something I could not wrap my head around. I had long ago abandoned the thought of talking about my abilities, and I knew no one would have ever believed me that Elvis was going to die.

While I was briefly convinced that I was imagining things, it wasn't until I started seeing confirmation of my psychic flashes that I realized what was happening was not going to go away. I now understand that the people I saw and got information about had to be in the public eye. It was the only way that the information that I had received could have been validated. If it had been a little-known Joe Smith from the next town over, I probably would never have known whether something had happened or not.

But the greater the validation, the more images flooded my brain, increasing to at least several times a week. I was bombarded by all this stimuli and didn't realize that my psychic channels were being overloaded. Moreover, everything that I had seen to date revolved around death—people who had crossed over or were getting ready for it.

Just what was I supposed to do with that exactly? How was I supposed to go out into the world and share what I was experiencing?

I felt embarrassed, ashamed; it was a dirty little secret that I felt I needed to hide. My mind kept trying to convince me that I really was crazy. Emotionally, it was too much for me to deal with.

So, I did what I felt I needed to do. I shut down. I prayed to God not to show me any more pictures or let me hear any voices. I told myself that I wasn't going to listen to or see anything that came way. My wish was definitely my command. Everything fell silent—at least for little while.

I Just Can't Run Away

Although it didn't seem like it at the time, my last two years of high school practically whizzed by. The focus at school was now on taking courses and achieving grades that would help you get into a post-secondary institution. It was almost a given that every person would be moving on to university or college, and so the educational environment was focused on looking to our futures. We were making choices and plans before any of us were legally adults.

I was surrounded by a myriad of voices, all trying to tell me which direction I was supposed to go in my life. I had to take French, because good jobs in Canada required it. I had to take algebra, because I never knew when I might need it in life. And I needed to take an archaic language such as Latin, because it would make me better rounded.

I struggled heavily with all of this. My mind was bored but also hyperactive. I had trouble sitting still, always wanting to turn around and talk to the person behind me. Because of the strict class regimen, I could not get up and move around the room whenever I wished. Once you sat in your seat, you stayed there for the whole class time. That was practically torture for me. I spent most of my time disinterested in class, not paying attention to what was being said. Doodles of artwork made their way throughout the pages of my books, but I didn't take notes. As a result, by the time twelfth grade rolled around, I was on the verge of failing many subjects.

In the midst of what I felt to be a dark place within me, a ray of hope came one day, in the form of a stranger—a stranger who became pivotal in my life, a stranger to whom I owe deep gratitude and hold dear in my heart.

While in the throws of my education, I was furthering my musical development through piano competitions and public performances. The pursuit of dance had ended when I was told by my ballet teacher that even though I was talented and expressive, I would never have a career as a ballerina. Apparently, I was too tall, too heavy, and my feet were too big. I lost interest and quit the expensive lessons. I still enjoyed performing though and pursued the one instrument that to me was a big escape from the pressures and chaos in all other areas of my life.

"Dr. M," as she came to be affectionately known, came into my life at one such piano competition. She was an adjudicator—a university professor who traveled throughout the province and provided expertise to budding musicians, much like judges at sports events or dance competitions. She was a strong supporter of talented, young artists and had great style and charisma. She was unlike any other judge I had encountered in all the years I had competed. Dr. M made a lasting impression on me.

She must have seen some potential in me, because after the weeklong competition, she approached me at the final concert. That was when all the festival winners had the opportunity to showcase their talents, strictly for performance purposes, without the pressure of competition.

Dr. M took a great interest in my musical talent and was the first person in my life who showed me that there was a future for me in the musical arena. It was a case of having someone come into your life at the right place and the right time. I truly believe in the concept of divine timing, and Dr. M was an example of synchronicity at its finest.

In between mouthfuls of food at the standard post-concert reception, Dr. M sat next to me and grilled me on what my plans were for post-secondary education. *What grade was I in? Had I thought about any specific universities?* I told her I hadn't thought about it whatsoever. Just like that, she told me that I had great talent, and she was interested in becoming my teacher. She sincerely hoped that I would consider attending Queen's University, in a small city in southern Ontario called Kingston. I was to look her up when I got there. Until that time, I hadn't known where Kingston was, much less thought about moving away from home.

But in that second, it was as if a bright light went off within me. I was amazed. Here was someone who had genuine interest in me and who believed in me. My view of my future changed in that moment. Suddenly I had something to grab hold of and move toward. I didn't know exactly how I would get there, but I knew instinctively that I had to eventually leave my town and be out on my own. The big hurdles were completing school satisfactorily and convincing my mother.

My mother's view of my future did not include my moving away from home. She wanted me to live at home, go to a local university, become a nurse, and get a good job. Everything was planned out for me. After the security of the job, then she would find a nice Ukrainian husband for me to settle down with and have a family. The career would be a backup in case something went wrong with the relationship.

Now that I had a glimpse of a potentially different future, the picture my mother painted for me turned me off. My strong will kicked in, and I was determined that I was not going to be put into someone else's box. I had a glimpse of a destination—I didn't know how or through what means I would get there, but my resolve was big enough that I was determined to create the new reality that was presented to me, no matter what the obstacles.

~ ~ ~

It was as if the Universe had stepped in and said, "Here you go Olena. Here's a different picture of life for you, and you can take it if you choose. So which are you going to choose?" One picture represented freedom; the other, oppression and constriction.

Over time, I discovered that on the road of life, it is virtually impossible to see the steps and the plan laid out in front of you. Chances are that you if you see all the steps, potentials, choices, consequences, and outcomes, they certainly don't belong to you. It's someone else's life. In other words, life's journey is like walking—you create the steps as you go along. And you can only see how far and where you have traveled, by looking backward, not forward.

The truth of that lay at the heart of my two opposing choices. The path that was shrouded headed toward the university and the person who would eventually become one of my greatest mentors. The path of constriction was the one laid out by my mother. That was her picture, her path, and her view of how she wanted my path to look. That was not the path I chose to travel.

From that point on, all I could think of was leaving. Time sped up, and everything inside of me felt like I needed to hurry to get somewhere. I was on the fast-track to making my new reality manifest exactly the way I saw it.

I started to put more effort into my studies, giving enough to make sure I passed and had sufficiently good grades to graduate. My friends that I had hung around with fell by the wayside. Thankfully, I hadn't developed an addiction to cigarettes and alcohol, and they lost their appeal. Suddenly I had a goal, and those people and their bad habits weren't in the picture. Graduating from Marymount was all I cared about, and I would do just about anything to get out.

And do just about anything, I did. So strong were my desires and intentions that I got expelled and had to finish my final six months of high school in the neighboring public coed high school. I didn't know that I was manifesting my great reality. But unconsciously, I did—and quickly too.

While I had let go of several bad choices, like smoking and drinking, I took on another. Marymount had a school lunch program. I lived too far away now to go home for lunch, so I brought along lunches that my mother made for me. Like many kids, I found that most of my brown-bag lunches were quite uninteresting.

My mother didn't believe in treats or the typical junk food items, so I never had anything like chips, pop, or candy in my lunch.

However, in the food department, I wasn't any different than other teenagers. I wanted to experience the "freedom" that I saw other girls have. Hot lunches required money. Money came from parents or family. But allowances were out of the question in my home. My mother didn't believe in giving children money. I would only get money when I got a job after completing post-secondary education, which of course would net me the "great job." Everything that I needed—food, clothing, and shelter—was taken care of for me. All I had to do was be the "good girl," be grateful that my necessities were taken care of, and concentrate on my schooling.

In general, I had no concept of the outside other than what I saw other girls go through. I wanted to be able to experience what it was like to have money of my own, to go up to the hot lunch line and buy something enjoyable. I wanted to have that bag of chips, that pop, or a candy bar. I envied the girls who miraculously pulled money out of their pockets, deposited it into the vending machines, and then munched away on their snacks during study period in the cafeteria. I wanted it so much that I would do just about anything to get it. So I did.

I decided I was going to help myself to some money—from my mother's purse. Although I wasn't fully aware of all the unconscious factors at work at the time, I was very angry with my mother. I was angry that she was so restrictive; I was angry for a whole host of reasons, none of which I could communicate through words.

When I work with people as a coach, I often mention that strong emotions such as anger or sadness cover a deep-seated and unfulfilled need inside of themselves. But children, no matter how old, aren't capable to really connect with those needs, especially when surrounded by dysfunctional living situations.

I had a need to be heard, to be deserving of attention, to be valued, to be acknowledged for who I was. I had lots of unfulfilled needs. I expressed them through actions rather than words.

A buck here. A buck there. At first, it didn't seem like a big deal. My mother would never know. Most of the time, she never paid attention to what I did or how I felt about anything. She would never miss that small of an amount, I reasoned. All I wanted was to feel gratified. And as with the other habits that I tried to adopt, I wanted to be accepted by my peers. I didn't want to be perceived as the odd man out at the lunch table, without only my brown-bag lunch.

One dollar led to five. Five led to ten. And ten led to twenty. Pretty soon I had traded a bad health habit for another, more serious one. This time, it was a habit that was turning me into a teenage criminal. I was of two minds at the time, however: one that knew what I was doing was wrong; the other that was carefree and reckless.

The recklessness won out. And it won me a ticket out of the school. My secret pilfering habit extended from home to school. I got caught stealing ten dollars from the instruction room of my music teacher, Sister Victoria. I was arrested and charged with minor theft. And in one quick moment, I had attention, but not the way I wanted it deep down.

My mother was furious. She wasted no time in telling me what an embarrassment I was to her and what people would think of her now as a parent. The arresting officer, a large, imposing man, told me that I was a con artist and needed to be in a juvenile detention center where I could be straightened out.

Sister Gloria, the principal, advised me that since my actions were not exemplary and not befitting the school, I would be expelled immediately. The judge I faced in court was thankfully lenient. According to him, I had temporarily lost my way and simply needed to get back on track. He advised me that he never wanted to see me in his courtroom again. And the school counselor, a gentle and sympathetic woman whom I saw just before being expelled, graciously informed me that I had HELP! written on my forehead in bold lettering. She asked me if I had anything to say about what I did. I looked her squarely in the eye and told her that I hated my mother and refused to live with her. That ended that conversation.

Just like that, I was out. I was seventeen. I finished the last six months of my education at the coed high school down the road, the very place that my mother had opposed. The shakeups just kept coming. My mother no longer financially supported anything I did. She stopped paying for my piano lessons, which by a miracle I continued. Sister Victoria, bless her wonderful soul, showed me the greatest amount of love and compassion, even though I had committed a grievous act in her room. She forgave me and continued to be my teacher without payment until I finished school and got into college.

My mother and I had a complete falling out. By this time, I had a loud voice inside just dying to come out. The extreme anger that had built up for years and my reckless behavior became a catalyst for a major change in the way I tapped into my own strength.

One day, during my adjustment to my new high school, I informed my mother that I was not planning to go to university locally. I had decided that I was going to Queens University, at least eight hours from home. I had taken the small, albeit shaky steps to controlling my life and had filled out the paperwork. Typically on college applications, you fill in your three choices of which schools you want to attend. I listed one. It was an absurd and risky move, but it never occurred to me that I would go any other place. The Universe was obviously on my side, because I was accepted. I informed my mother on a day when she was in her usual tentative mood swing. My declaration infuriated her. As her anger rose, so did her voice. I rose to the challenge. I finally stood up for myself.

My voice only provoked my mother further. As she raised her hand to strike me, somewhere deep inside of me, a new strength surged. As she started to aim, my hand shot out and stopped her. By this time, I was taller and towered over her. I firmly held her arm and told her that it was the last time that she would ever hit me. She must have realized I was serious, because she never touched me again. But in that moment, something snapped inside of me. It was if I had shifted something deep within me, and a new person was emerging.

By the time I got to school that day, I felt as if I were in another realm. I never made it to first class. I stood by my locker, slightly shaken by what had occurred earlier that morning with my mother. A voice inside of me prompted me to get to the school pay phone and call an aunt, who lived in the vicinity. My mother had ostracized herself from the rest of my relatives—her siblings—so my aunt was aware of the growing tumultuousness in my household. I told her that I needed a place to stay for awhile and explained that morning's situation.

I had no intention of going back home. Frankly, I was flying by the seat of my pants, but I didn't care. It was the end of what I knew as home. Who knew that that morning would be my last time in my own bed? God must have known, because in hindsight I had help all along the way. In less than a month, I had removed myself from a school I disliked, a home that wasn't really my home, and a mother with whom I had a tumultuous relationship. And I hadn't even reached my eighteenth birthday.

I was serious about never returning home. I had only the clothes on my back when I left. I had no money to call my own, no life skills, and no sense of what I was going to do. My mother begged me to come back. Apologizing for her behavior, she said she was willing to do anything for me, even pay for my post-secondary education, but on the condition that I come back home. I stood my ground. Even though I was torn with sadness, my inner strength gained new footing.

I never saw or spoke to my mother again. What few possessions I had were stuffed in a box and shipped to my aunt's house. It was as if the Universe was telling me that all of this was in the past, and I was to leave everything that wasn't needed anymore behind.

Overall, good things happened. I reconnected with my father, whom I hadn't seen for more than nine years. I graduated from high school, and by a miracle, I auditioned for my soon-to-be-mentor in Kingston, who remembered me immediately from our meeting several years earlier. I got accepted into a specialized music performance program. I left the city, leaving everything from that chapter of life behind. I was on my way.

I'm Here to Do—What?

CHAPTER SIX

If people offer their help or wisdom as you go through life, accept it gratefully. You can learn much from those who have gone before you. But never be afraid or hesitant to step off the accepted path and head off in your own direction, if your heart tells you that it's the right way for you. Always believe that you will ultimately succeed at whatever you do, and never forget the value of persistence, discipline, and determination. You are meant to be whatever you dream of becoming.[6]

—Edmund O'Neill
American author

Just like that, I was a college freshman. If somebody had asked me how I would have envisioned my life up until that point, I never would have thought that I could endure and experience so much in such a short time. Eighteen years of being alive isn't much time in the grand scheme of things, yet I had been through a lot: I was a talented pianist and veteran performer; I had witnessed and experienced abuse all around me; I was an amateur psychic-medium; and I had the guts to walk out on my mother and the safety of my own home all within two short decades of life. But the freedom of being on my own and walking my own path, despite the fears, challenges, and hurdles that went with it, overrode everything.

I discovered that if I pursued something I enjoyed, my grades improved, and I was more motivated to learn and explore my inner self in the process. Until then,

I hadn't really figured out who I was as a person. I had been simply doing what I needed to do to survive.

The beauty of being in post-secondary education was that most people were there for the same reasons. The environment was so different from high school. In high school, there was a tendency for students to form groups and cliques. Once you leave high school, those become less significant. The stakes are much higher. Post-secondary education costs money. Very little is taken for granted because of the investment involved. Few students have time for cliques and segregation, because most are there for the learning and achievement.

I matured at the university. I was surrounded by people who didn't know me or my past and accepted me for who I was. All around me were musicians, with various degrees of ambition—some serious, some not so. For once I felt like a normal person, without having to please anyone or buy my friendships. And that was freeing.

I enjoyed my classes at university. It was a privilege and an honor to be chosen as one of a small handful of students in Dr. M's specialized performance program. That meant high standards and expectations, and as a musician I was constantly pushed to stretch beyond my comfort zone.

For the first year, I did nothing but immerse myself in my studies. I lived in a quiet dormitory across the street from the building where I had my music classes. I discovered that all my years of music and dance training paid off in the discipline department. Because of the high expectations, I had to practice whenever I could.

Competition for practice space was high, so I found myself burning the candle at both ends—going to bed at midnight and getting up at 5:30 AM to practice in the quiet halls of the music building for several hours until the flurry of students started several hours later. Getting less than six hours of sleep per night was routine. I think that discipline gave me great training for later in life when I became a mother.

Even though university life was enjoyable, it was still stressful, and my anxiety levels rose, mainly because I didn't have a support system. At least I didn't have to cook for myself, because I was living in a dormitory. I had the luxury of eating in a dining hall with unlimited food at my disposal.

To compensate for my stress, my high school habit of eating junk food, mostly sweets, returned with a vengeance. I also started drinking coffee every morning to cope with the lack of sleep. Because I was always in a hurry to get enough practice time in before my early classes, I rushed through an unbalanced breakfast, sometimes skipping it entirely. I was always hyperactive, and my quest for high achievement was very important. Adrenaline, I discovered, was something I thrived on, and the more energy I had, the better.

Most mornings I subsisted on toasted English muffins, coffee, and grapefruit juice—something that I could eat in ten minutes or less. I convinced myself that spending time to eat, especially in the mornings, was a waste of my time. But by lunch and dinner I was starving and gave myself full reign to eat as much as I wanted. I would freely take second helpings of the main course along with unlimited desserts, and then more coffee to get me through the evening study period.

I believed that the more extremes that I went to, the better success I would have in everything I was involved in. I also reasoned that because I was expending so much energy practicing my instrument, that I was eating more to refuel. It quickly caught up with me. By the end of my first year at college, I was fifty pounds overweight, had developed chronic migraines and anxiety, and a stomach ulcer. I was unmotivated, and my wardrobe no longer fit. I lived in my two pairs of jeans with loose-fitting shirts and sweaters to cover up my growing waistline.

My first summer away from home was daunting. It was also the start of several powerful wakeup calls in my life. While most students disappeared over the summer, usually to go home and find jobs, I was one of the few who stayed on campus. Since I had no home to go back to, a source of great sadness for me, I fended for myself. While my education was supported mostly by student loans and somewhat by my father, who had come back into my life, I still needed to earn some money.

I got several jobs working as a waitress and found a fairly inexpensive room to rent in a house that belonged to a professor. The discovery that I had a great deal of ambition inside of me came as a surprise. During the summer, I decided to get a jump-start on my elective courses. That way, I could devote my energies to my music specialty during the regular school year. Here I finally had the freedom to choose what I wanted and how to go about achieving it.

I enrolled in creative writing and learned how to craft a screenplay. I thought creative writing would be easy, yet enjoyable. I had always loved to write, and this was a chance for my expression to come through. I was intrigued with learning to writing a screenplay. I had always wanted to do theater and dramatic arts, but my mother considered it unbecoming for a young girl. So I never got involved with theater while I lived at home. But during the last summer before I left for university I starred in a local production of *Annie*. The thought of being an actress grabbed my attention. I loved to sing and dance on stage and discovered that I had a flair for it. Although I never seriously pursued it after that, it was a good experience for me to be on a stage and become comfortable in front a large group of people.

Between my writing classes, jobs, and struggles with my weight and health, I was tired and overwhelmed. One part of me was ambitious and driven; the other simultaneously struggled with boredom, lethargy, and depression. It was during my episodes of depression that I encountered Shirley MacLaine and two of her books—*Out on a Limb* and *Dancing in the Light*.

The Awakening

I was sitting alone in the house where I rented a room one very hot afternoon, not knowing how I was going to entertain myself. The professor who owned the house had an extensive collection of books. I was an avid reader, so I gravitated to the bookshelf. Shirley MacLaine caught my eye. It was like I was pulled toward her books by some unseen force. From the moment I opened them, I was hooked. Both *Out on a Limb* and *Dancing in the Light* were stories about Shirley's personal psychic experiences and awakening.

I devoured the books, entranced with the notion of channeling, talking to spirits (aka mediumship), and uncovering one's own psychic abilities. Moreover, I admired her for having the courage to write about herself and her experiences for anyone to read—in other words, to expose herself to potential criticism as well as support. Caught up at the same time in the energy of my creative writing course, I remember thinking that I could write a book just like Shirley's. Somewhere inside of me I knew that was something I could do. I aspired to be a writer like Shirley. I wanted to write about mind-body-spirit topics too, especially my own experiences growing up as an intuitive child.

One book led to another. I found myself delving into all things esoteric and spiritual, but I favored those that had a biographical bent. Among my favorites were J. Z. Knight's *A State of Mind: My Story* and any of Edgar Cayce's books on spirit communication and channeling, past life information, and meditation techniques. I became a sponge. I wanted to learn everything connected with the spiritual. What I had shut down in high school was quickly reopening. I was hungry for information. I not only wanted to learn but also wanted to experience.

That desire manifested itself quickly after my declaration of what I wanted. I found and joined a local meditation group. I enjoyed the group, especially the social aspect and coming of like minds, but I wanted more. One of the women in the group, Anne, was a practicing psychic and taught psychic development and mediumship courses. I inquired about the classes and found that they were affordable, even on my limited budget as a working student. I promptly enrolled in her course. Now I was juggling three courses and two jobs! At least I was doing what I found myself drawn toward, and that lessened any sense of being overwhelmed.

Anne taught me many of the mechanical aspects of the psychic arts and spirituality—chakras or energy centers in the body (see chapter 13 for more details), energy fields, and auras. I learned how an aura was comprised of different layers and held different types of information. I learned that this was what psychics usually tapped into when "reading" a person. Different modes of psychic communication and reception of information were addressed. I learned that I was strong on many of the "clairs" (which means "clear"). I was primarily clairaudient— or clear hearing. Many of my early experiences where I "heard" a voice in my head were actually my clairaudient channel wide open. That was quickly followed by clairvoyance and clairsentience—visual and feeling/emotional.

This validated for me that what I had encountered throughout my childhood was not made up. It was not in my imagination. I was certainly not crazy, and here was someone who understood where I was at. For the first time, I had hope that there was something to all of this.

Anne was also a medium, which means that she was able to connect with spirit beings that were once here on earth in body and had crossed over. Anne taught me that there were mental and physical forms of mediumship. She helped me discover that many of the mediumship encounters I had had with my family members or friends were considered a form of mental mediumship. That means that I was connecting or making contact with a spirit utilizing my "clairs": clairaudience, clairvoyance, clairsentience, and claircognizance.

Psychic readings and conducting mediumship sessions were my favorite parts of the class. Even though it was unnerving for me to sit down formally with someone, I took up the challenge as I had in other parts of my life. I was finally starting to do something with what was naturally a part of me. Where this was headed I still did not know, but the summer of 1986 was definitely a wakeup for me.

Shifts Happen

It was my second year of university. They call it the "make or break" year. That means that how you do academically in this year makes a difference in whether you continue forward with your post-secondary or graduate education or drop out. My educational standards were suddenly raised. Much more was expected of me at this stage, and the levels of stress increased. At least my body was lighter. In addition to my summertime activities, I had enforced a strict exercise and diet regime on myself—jogging, aerobics, working out to Jane Fonda, and switching to a no-sugar, low-fat, vegetarian diet. I was still a coffee junkie, though! Nevertheless, the excess pounds melted off. Within four months, I had lost almost sixty pounds. I looked better and definitely felt better than I had in a long time.

I returned to school with great anticipation. Something in me had changed. I was now in a hurry to continue forward with my studies, even though my inner awareness had shifted to something that I just couldn't identify. I plunged into my studies with fervor. Going to extremes once again became my modus operandi. After my weight gain, I developed a fear of going through that again, so I reduced my food consumption drastically, thinking that the less I ate the less I would gain. I fell back into extreme eating, or non-eating, extreme practicing, and burning the candle at both ends.

I was two months shy of end-of-year performance (every music student in the performance program had to give a year-end, juried concert, the success of which was the deciding factor for entry into the senior years) when I burned out. I hadn't learned what balance meant and how to pace myself. My arms and fingers were so overworked that I developed tendonitis in both arms. Tendonitis is an inflammation of the tendons due to strain or overwork. It practically crippled me. I was forced to stop consistent practice for about a month. The future of my career as a professional concert pianist hung in the balance.

The break helped somewhat. It was enough to get me back on track for the end of the year. In the middle of my preparations for the performance, a bomb dropped in my lap. My father, who had been supporting me financially, retired. There would be no more money coming from him. My student loans also were running dry, and it was too late to apply for new ones. Once again, I was faced with surviving on my own. This added to the growing stress I was already undergoing. The timing couldn't have been worse. I was faced with tough choices and decisions to make. But I was a survivor, and somewhere deep within I drew on that and never gave up.

I passed my performance with flying colors. Unknown to me, it was to be my last major performance. There was no money for me to continue going to school, and I saw no reason to register for my remaining years until I had the money to do so. Luckily, I learned that I did not have to drop out. I could postpone one year of university and return without losing anything other than time.

Allowing myself only a brief time to feel sorry for myself, I took the opportunity of a yearlong break. I had to rethink what this situation was trying to tell me. *Maybe what looked like chaos was really a blessing in disguise. Did that mean that maybe I wasn't cut out for the concert pianist circuit? Was there more to the plan than I thought?* My spiritual learning had taught me that everything happens for a reason, and maybe this was the Universe's way of gently telling me that this wasn't really my path after all. I had undoubtedly created the tendonitis so I could get a loud wake-up call.

But I needed money to survive, so I did what I needed to do. Drawing on my hardworking farming family's work ethic, I got two jobs—one working five days a week as a cashier in a local supermarket and the second as an organist at a local church on Sundays. Both were no-brainer jobs for me. After all, I was working only to pay my living expenses until I figured out what exactly I was supposed to do in my life and save up enough money to get through the next two school years. It was a temporary measure. After all, I still had a greater vision for my life.

I gained a great sense of freedom and relief. Even though I had my working obligations, it was an interesting feeling being on your own and only having yourself to be responsible for. Because I had a lot more flexibility than my twelve-hour days of school, I was able to explore, think, meditate, and discover myself. My heart called me back to Anne's meditation group from the previous summer. I decided that I needed to return to listening to my inner nudgings. *Perhaps there was something to that quiet little voice after all*, I surmised.

One night, I decided to get an official reading from Anne. In her sessions, it was typical for the reader to sit across from the person being read, typically called the sitter or just the client. Because Anne knew me previously from her psychic development class, she didn't need to hold my hand or a personal object of mine to tune in to my energy. I simply sat across from her while she focused on my energy field and connected with the angelic realm and the Universal Energy which some call God. Within seconds, she began to impart information about what she was seeing. Anne was primarily clairvoyant, and all of her readings were based on what she saw and heard. She first looked at my aura and described all the colors that she saw around me. I had a mixture of green, pink, purple, and gold around my head, but specifically dark blue that emanated from my soul, she said.

Inwardly I gasped. That was exactly what I had found when I had taken the quiz from the book *What Color is Your Aura?* a year earlier. The dark blue was the color of Indigo, and it was significant of someone very energetically sensitive and psychic. Practically reading my mind, Anne went on to say that I had several angels, spirit guides, and deceased people around me who had come forward from the spirit realm. Apparently it was a big crowd that had arrived to talk to me, Anne said with a smile. I was mesmerized.

Suddenly I had flashbacks to my earlier days where I saw and communicated with spirits but ended up shutting down for fear that no one would understand, or worse, would label me as crazy. There was one person in particular who wanted to give me a message. And that came as a great shock to me. It was something I never expected. The person was a young girl named Nita, a girl I knew from high school.

In June of 1985, Nita had died during the bombing of Air India Flight 182. Nita and I were not close friends, but we had had a friendly relationship. I remember saying good-bye to her and giving her a farewell hug on graduation day. I felt sad at the thought of not seeing her again, but chalked it up to the typical feelings of letting go as people move in different directions in their lives. Two days later, I found out from another friend that Nita was on the Air India flight, going to spend the summer with her family. I was in disbelief. It was my first experience of a major tragedy where someone I knew died, especially someone so young. It was so shocking to me that in the moment I received the news, I realized that life truly was short, and the end of it could happen at any time. I needed to make the best of it.

That was exactly the message that came through in my session with Anne. I hadn't connected with Nita in spirit since her passing. I had effectively closed down my channels for receiving spirit communication, because I was too fearful. Now I couldn't run away from that anymore. Nita told me that everyone on this earth was here for a purpose, and that life itself was short. I needed to discover why I was here, because there was great work to be done, and my contribution to this planet was important.

It took me a while to digest that information. Anne proceeded to tell me that one of my purposes was to write. *There it was again!* The writing theme. No matter how much I tried, I couldn't get away from that. During my psychic development course, we had also learned about the Akashic Records.

The Akashic Records are essentially a large database about every living being. Every soul being's existence was recorded—every thought, word, action, choices, and decisions prior to incarnating into a human body. That included our purpose, our mission, agreements that we made with others to learn specific lessons on earth, an overall life theme that we chose to work on while in human body, and a skeletal life plan that we chose to design.

Anne said that my soul had "writer" stamped all over it. As I sat there and thought about it, I realized that this theme had showed itself from the very beginning of my life. From the moment I became aware of it as a mere five-year-old sitting at a typewriter in kindergarten, it replayed itself throughout my life. It was like a flag waving inside of me every now and then, letting me know when I had strayed too far from the course that I, as a soul, had already planned for myself.

Anne also told me that I was very psychic, and one of my biggest gifts was as a medium and transitional worker, helping people cross over to the other side after this life. She said that one of my angelic guides was Archangel Rafael, and that my aura had a lot of green, which was indicative of being both a healer and a teacher of children. Archangel Rafael, one of the four major archangels in the Judeo-Christian religions, also assists people with their clairvoyant abilities.

I was allowed to ask questions during the reading. One of my curiosities surrounded a relationship that I was in. During the summer of 1986, I had met and started dating another university student named Arnold. I wanted to know where this relationship was headed. Anne told me that she saw me getting married to this man and having children. The children were especially important. She said that my children would have a special place in this world, and I was a guardian of these children.

The reading astounded me. I had not expected any of the information so far, but I had come into the reading with an open mind, which was probably the best thing to do. The messages and the pictures that she saw and received were so different from what my life looked like at that time.

I didn't know how to reconcile those two. I was on hiatus from university. My professor had expectations that I would return and complete my studies. That vision was that I would be a professional concert pianist. I walked away from the reading confused.

Was I supposed to be a professional psychic? Writer? Healer?

The last thing I wanted to do was be a professional psychic—visions of dark-skinned women wrapped in shawls in dimly lit rooms hovering over crystal balls frankly scared the heck out of me. No way was I going to be like that! And my only experience with writers was that they wrote fiction or children's books and occasionally biographies like the ones that I read. I didn't see myself writing fiction or children's books. And healer meant being a nurse or a doctor, going through more years of post-secondary education, all of which required more and more money that I just didn't have.

My belief system at the time was that I needed to work. I needed to make money to survive. And *then* I could think about my life. I remembered a book that I had read the year before, *The Amazing Laws of Cosmic Mind Power* by Dr. Joseph Murphy. What I gleaned from the book was the concept that I was the creator of my life, and what I thought, said, and believed shaped my reality. But if I had also chosen as a soul to be a writer in this lifetime and had a mission to teach, heal, or work with children, then obviously what I was creating in that very moment was not in sync with what I had pre-planned for myself prior to being here.

Anne told me that it was important to follow my heart. The heart was the gateway of the soul, and my soul expressed itself and communicated through my feelings. If something didn't feel right, then it was probably not the right thing to do. If the feelings were uplifting, then that was a clue that I was on the right course. I listened to her and took her advice.

That same week, I was sitting in my doctor's office waiting for my weekly ultrasound treatment for my ongoing tendonitis problem. I was leafing through magazines and spotted a local college catalog. I pored through the catalog. Training to become a paralegal caught my eye. I had always been intrigued by law, especially legal philosophy. A course in law had been offered as an extracurricular course when I was in grade twelve. I had wanted to take it, but my mother vetoed the option, suggesting that this was not something I should focus on.

Staring at the course description, I reasoned that this training would get me a decent job in a law office. In Ontario, paralegals could attend court and deal with minor aspects of legal cases, usually in front of justices of the peace. I loved that idea. I decided quickly that since my energy was being drawn to it, this was probably something I needed to do. Wherever this took me, I would follow it. I got a student loan and signed up for the program.

But my university degree was still unfinished, hanging in midair. I inquired about what I needed to complete my degree and discovered that I could enroll in the minimum number of courses while I was also enrolled in the paralegal course.

Suddenly I was attending both university and college at the same time. Somehow, I managed it all.

Overall, I loved the paralegal training. I not only learned about the law, I became enthralled by it. I loved it so much that I decided I wanted to become a lawyer and pursue family law, dealing with divorce cases and children. Shades of my own broken childhood were definitely prevalent. About halfway through my training, I had an opportunity to do something new. The English as a Second Language (ESL) department at the college recruited the top students in the paralegal training to help teach students English. This would be a paid position, and I jumped at the chance. Anything to expand myself, I thought. This would give me great experience working with young people.

The teacher of the ESL program, Jean McGovern, had to train us to get all of her interns, as she called us, prepared to teach foreign students. Part of her training included intensive writing classes, including creative writing as well as more formalized learning about grammar and syntax. All of her students were supposed to keep an ongoing journal of their experiences and continuously engage in writing exercises that would liberate our creativity.

Jean was a positive person, always encouraging her students to take their writing seriously. She would tell us that everyone had a voice, and that we all had something to say in our lives. It didn't matter whether we would be famous novelists or someone who journaled privately. It was important to recognize that we were unique, and that our voices mattered, no matter how they were expressed.

Jean would often comment on my writing. I felt unsure of myself most of the time, embarrassed that I was sharing my innermost feelings and thoughts with my teacher. The last thing that she wrote to me on our final day of training was that she thought I was a great writer and that she could see me write amazing things one day. Her opinion was that I needed to just do it. *Keep writing*, she said, *and never quit.*

I took those words to heart. But unfortunately, that is where they stayed for awhile. Jean was instrumental in triggering the idea that everything was possible, and she believed in us as creative artists, but I didn't sit down to write anything significant for another three years. It was a struggle in the meantime.

One day I had the inspiration that I could write a book. I sat down in front of my typewriter, thinking that all I had to do was sit, and the words would come. I reasoned that if writing was my purpose, all I had to do was tap into that, and then everything would be easy. I would just churn out the Great Canadian Novel.

But alongside the momentary inspirational moments, was the critical voice in my head saying, *What on earth would you write about? You have nothing to say. That isn't a career. You can't make a living from this. Who are you? Somebody special?*

I rolled the paper into the machine and sat there. I thought about what I could write. Mentally, I made a list of the types of books I loved to read—biographies, spiritual topics, psychic development, and romantic stories. Joan always advised her students that we should write about what we knew. *Perhaps I could write about myself,* I thought. That would be something I knew well enough. I could start there. But nothing came. There was just me and the loud critical voice. I gave in to the voice. In less than five minutes, my first attempt at writing what I thought was something really big ended. What I wasn't fully cognizant of was that I didn't believe in myself. I allowed myself to believe that the loud, critical voice was right. It said that I didn't have anything important to say.

I quit right then and there, determining that this was a waste of my time. However, my soul wouldn't let me off the hook that easily. I found out that in life, although you may try and stray from the path and ignore what your soul is trying to communicate, your soul will always gently nudge you back and remind you that you are off track. I've come to the conclusion that we can never finish our lives until our personal mission and life purpose are fulfilled. So you might as well listen as early as possible.

The Indigo Has Landed

It was 1990. I completed both my music studies at the university and paralegal course at another local college practically at the same time. I got married to Arnold and moved to the West Coast of Canada. A new chapter in my life had begun. I settled down to the day-to-day business of survival. For the first four years, I survived—only. My first job was as a paralegal in a civil litigation firm, dealing mostly with motor vehicle accident victims and injury claims. I enjoyed the subject matter and found individual cases fascinating, but I longed for something meatier like family, marriage, and divorce cases.

Other parts of the job frustrated me. I didn't enjoy the structure of a nine-to-five job. Watching the lawyers have the freedom to come and go as they pleased sparked resentment inside of me. I felt stuck in a system that didn't suit me. For several years, I grumbled about it. And then the Universe stepped in.

Within four years of being a paralegal, I held three different jobs. I got fired from each one. Ironically though, I was not fired because I was doing a bad job.

Just the opposite. Every employer gave me nothing but glowing reports on my work. But each time, the reasons for letting me go were that I spoke out too much and created controversy and upheaval. There was no room for someone in a supporting position with strong opinions. After the third firing, I finally got the message.

Instead of rushing into yet another job, I listened to myself. Following my heart was vital. There were too many instances in my past in which I hadn't done that. Each time I went down a road that I thought was right, something happened. The Universe was showing me, whether through being fired or having opportunities come up like the ESL class, that I wasn't paying enough attention to my calling. By so doing, I was paying disservice to my soul. I decided to rest, relax, and spend some time in introspection.

First, I took stock of myself and my character. I realized that I wasn't cut out for a structured job, and I wasn't to working for another person. I didn't enjoy being told when I could eat, take a break, get up, sit down, or anything else. I didn't take instruction well from other people; it restricted my freedom. I preferred to set and follow my own rules. I also wanted to deeply understand why people made the choices that they did, and why they behaved in certain ways.

That was why I wanted to work in family law. Understanding human behavior was compelling. My own dysfunctional family life was the impetus for this deep, inner longing. I wanted to understand the core of people. *If people made different choices, if they chose different thoughts or actions, would those decisions have a completely different effect on their behavior, their physical well-being, and their outlook on life?* I wondered. The seeds of the mind-body-spirit connection were being planted, thanks to my time off.

My health had also deteriorated again during this time. It was a relief not to be working for awhile. Several years earlier, I had been diagnosed with both fibromyalgia and adult attention deficit hyperactivity disorder (ADHD). I started making strong mind-body connections between the environments I was in, the choices I made, and how they affected my body, emotions, and mind. The longer I stayed in the nine-to-five job and stressful situations such as the fast-paced law office, the more pain my body experienced and the unhappier I became. According to my doctor, I was also suffering from chronic fatigue syndrome. Total rest and removal from all stressful environments was prescribed. It couldn't have come at a better time. And it gave me a much needed wakeup call.

I took action. I stopped going to see medical doctors, because they were giving me more and more medication. The increase in medication, I concluded, was adding to my physical illness. I chose not to pollute my body with synthetics anymore. Good health became a priority. I threw away my medication, and started on a whole-body cleanse. Due to many years of living next to two major train tracks and metal mines, coupled with having had braces on my teeth for five years, it was determined by a naturopathic physician my body was full of heavy metals. I was allergic to many foods, especially processed foods, as well as synthetic clothing fibers and products. I couldn't wear anything metallic or mechanical, not even a watch. Loud noises made me feel worse. All of those things drained my energy.

Alternative medicine became my preferred mode of healing. Many visits to herbalists, energy workers, and naturopathic physicians helped me to see that my own unhappiness and disconnection from my soul calling were contributing to my physical and emotional pain. And I needed to that level of pain to see how disconnected I had become.

So I read, researched, and studied as many healing modalities as I could. Eventually I took a leap of faith and opened my own health clinic, The Mind-Body Connection Centre. My soul was calling me to educate people about their own mind-body-spirit disconnection and to help them know themselves in a deeper way.

I do believe that life is like a big jigsaw puzzle. All the pieces are there, but we need to rearrange them to discover the whole picture. When the pieces fall into place in one's soul, there are angels in heaven who sing for joy. The feeling of finally "getting it" is glorious.

For me, that moment occurred when my depression lifted, and both my fibromyalgia and chronic fatigue disappeared. Living in my authenticity energized my soul. I realized that working for other people and being in structured jobs, under the rules of others, had been killing my soul. And the farther away I walked from my purpose and mission in life, the more painfully obvious it became in my body and my emotions. I finally had made my own mind-body connection.

The clinic expanded to include spiritual healing and related components. It was a tenuous place to be. Where I lived, the concept of mind and body connection was fairly new. And the belief that we are what we think was considered outlandish by many. Spirit itself didn't really have much of a place. Yet, it was an integral piece of the puzzle. If I didn't acknowledge that, I would yet again be doing my soul a disservice.

I was already advertising my business in a few major New Age and health magazines. Taking a large gulp, I proposed to the editors of a couple of journals that I write some articles for them. To my surprise, they agreed. At first, I wrote on various health topics and stuck to physical healing modalities. But that didn't do it all justice. The more I wrote, the more my soul nudged me to expand and do more. I was delving into the spirit world again.

One day I was speaking to the editor of a New Age publication about my latest article, when she asked me if I had ever thought about teaching classes on psychic development. We had had many conversations about intuitive work, angels, and healing, so when she approached me about this, I wasn't too surprised. I could feel my soul practically leap out of my chest at the thought of delving back into the spiritual world.

Me—teaching?

Almost immediately the critical voice that had followed me around for years crept back in, nagging me with negatives.

I wasn't an expert in this. What credentials did I have to teach someone how to open their intuitive channels? I was a fraud. Nobody will accept me.

On and on, the voice went. But this time, I was ready for it. I knew it for what it was. The critical voice was a good teacher, simply letting me know that the closer I got to my purpose, the more resistance I would feel. That's how I would know. If the critical voice showed up, I must be doing something of value and purposeful. What a great lesson for me!

My intuitive channels were back in full swing. I started facilitating basic classes and workshops on angel connection, introductory psychic development classes, and more advanced channeling classes such as mediumship and soul readings. My own experiences as well as angelic guidance shaped the material for the classes. Sometimes I would have one person, other times I had as many as a dozen people in my classes. In the end, everything was perfect. Many times the class material took on a life of its own. It was if I were creating the class on the spot. But I so enjoyed it. It gave me a sense of fulfillment.

I came out of the closet as a practicing intuitive. All of my years of performing music prepared me for being in the public eye. I found myself attracting more opportunities for being visible. Several television shows contacted me about being on their programs about psychic healing and work. Although I was nervous, I took on every opportunity that came my way. I resolved never to ignore my inner calling again, no matter how fearful I felt.

Somewhere in the middle of all this, the Indigo concept reappeared. I had been exposed to it in 1986 when the book *What Color Is Your Aura* practically fell on my head. I knew that I resonated to the color Indigo, but up until the mid-nineties I didn't fully integrate the characteristics consciously into my life. Almost nobody had heard of Indigos at that time, or at least no one proclaimed it out loud. It wasn't until my daughter was born, that I had the courage to proclaim it, loud and clear.

My daughter, Katerina, was born in 1996. She is a Crystal child. She is very psychic and made no bones about showing it from the beginning. Katerina visited me several times before her conception. When I say visit, I mean a spirit visit, usually in a dream state. I was told quite clearly that it was important that I accept who I was, and that I needed to expose my "blue body." I couldn't hide that part of me anymore. What the "blue body" referred to was my spirit body (more on the subject of bodies in the section on auras). Ironically, in *What Color is Your Aura?* the perfect complement to an Indigo is a Crystal. They get along famously. Given what I know now about the Indigo way of being, it's no wonder that the Crystal children are the next wave of Super Sensitives, and many are being born to Indigo parents.

It was my daughter who fully brought the pieces of being Indigo home for me. Although I was fully aware that I had something great to accomplish in this life, I also knew that part of that involved being a guardian to a special child. This didn't just come from Anne's reading many years earlier. In my soul, this was a mission, a serious mission, not one to be taken casually. To be able to help a Super Sensitive child navigate her way in this world, a world in chaos, upheaval, and great change, it was vital that I knew who I was in all ways.

At the age of thirty, I came home—home to myself. I'm sure the angels in heaven were cheering and having a celebration that day. I had chosen my life, both created and yet to be created. I had chosen my parents, my family, and the people around me growing up. I had chosen seemingly negative experiences to learn quickly and accelerate into and wake up to who I really was. I say seemingly, because I believe that chaos and opportunity are two sides of the same coin, as the Chinese expression goes. I had chosen experiences that helped me realize that I couldn't find myself through external sources or substances. I had to learn that no matter how hard you try to ignore or run away from who you are, you will always gently be pulled back. In other words, you cannot run away from your Indigo self, regardless of how chaotic and difficult the experiences around you seem to be.

Indigos big or small, you are all here for a reason. You have a job to do. You have a mission and purpose to fulfill. Perhaps some of you will have to be in the process for awhile, to wake up to your full self. That is perfectly okay. Age is irrelevant. You are who you are. And that unto itself is enough.

RAISING THE AWARENESS
Understanding the Super Sensitive

PART II

Indigos, Crystal, and Cusps—Oh My!

CHAPTER SEVEN

If help and salvation are to come, they can only come from the children, for the children are the makers of men.[7]

—Maria Montessori
Italian educator and psychologist

What was your first thought when you read the above title? What was your reaction to the word *Indigo? Crystal? Cusp?* Do they resonate with you? Or are you wondering what on earth you're reading? These are terms that have in the last several years been making their way into our homes, onto the Internet, into workshops, onto television, and into our lives, fast becoming household terms.

It's true. These *are* terms. Human beings need words. We need specific terms, because our understanding of concepts is directly tied into specific distinctions. Our brains enjoy categorizing. Using distinctive terms caters to the compartmentalization in which we engage consistently. These terms allow us to communicate thoughts and ideas to others verbally, trusting that the words used mean the same to the speaker and the listener. Indigos, Crystals, and Cusps are terms to describe distinctive groups of beings. Again, for ease of understanding, I will refer to this whole group as the "Super Sensitive."

Large numbers of Super Sensitives are children, and in smaller numbers, adults. All are awakening to the knowledge that they are somehow "different" than many people, but they don't necessarily know why. They are aware that they don't fit well into our society and are having challenges navigating through life. If you have reached this point in this book, chances are you are a parent, caregiver, or educator of such a child, or you are a Super Sensitive yourself.

While it may seem that these "new" terms are pervading our lives, the phenomenon of the Super Sensitive is not new at all. Scattered throughout the history of mankind, there have been many Super Sensitive people walking the planet. The difference between then and now is that larger numbers are here. It has become much more noticeable in the last three or four decades, but especially in the last decade. (In chapter 9, I will delve more deeply into this.)

To explain the terminology, Indigos and Crystals were originally named for the connection between the color of one's aura and distinctive characteristics relating to behavior, personality, and character. In 1982, parapsychologist Nancy Tappe coined the terms "Indigo" and "Crystal" in *Understanding Your Life through Color*. Barbara Bowers, who wrote *What Color Is Your Aura*, also linked color with physical, emotional, and spiritual characteristics.

The names Indigo, Crystal, Indigo-Crystal, and Cusp refer not so much to an aura color as to a color that resonates and emanates through the soul. Color is merely vibration—different colors are different frequencies or blends of frequencies of light. Imagine a rainbow, ranging from red on one end to violet on the other, each ray of color having its own frequency.

As humans, we emanate frequency and vibration. The spectrum of Super Sensitive is really the embodiment of specific rays of color or vibration, the full spectrum of which is emanating from and through the soul. In fact, one can further distinguish these rays: within the Indigo or Crystal ray, you can have various combinations or blends, such as Violet/Indigo or Indigo/Crystal.

The specific vibration of the Super Sensitive is directly connected to a specific purpose in life—both personal and global. For example, while there are thousands of Indigos, each will have his or her unique purpose and method of expression, giving an individualized personality spectrum.

Throughout the initial development of this book, I had many people write and e-mail me to ask me how they could really know if they or someone they knew were Indigos, especially if they couldn't read auras or people's energy. My simple answer was that if they had reached the point of reading and posting their queries, chances are they simply required external validation to what they already knew internally.

Because the identification of Super Sensitive is primarily intangible—being an energetic resonance of the soul—it is imperative to look at the external and concrete. This includes specific personality and behavioral patterns, as well as traits and characteristics in various categories of our lives.

I have developed a questionnaire to cater to the curious mind and the need for external validation. My hope is that this may be one way of achieving a better insight and more expansive understanding of the Super Sensitive. The purpose of these questionnaires is to help you see whether you, your child, or someone you know resonates to Super Sensitive energy. It is a not test to see whether you pass or fail. There is no good or bad, right or wrong, better or worse. This is simply about discovery, understanding, and perhaps with some of you, confirmation of what you already knew to begin with. Have fun!

The Indigo/Crystal Questionnaires

CHAPTER EIGHT

Children are a wonderful gift... They have an extraordinary capacity to see into the heart of things and to expose sham and humbug for what they are.[8]

—Desmond Tutu
Archbishop of Capetown, South Africa and activist

Is Your Child an Indigo?

Note: This questionnaire is adaptable for parents, caregivers, and educators.

Does your child:

1. *Get impatient easily and consistently?*
   Yes _____ No _____

2. *Have a strong will and temperament?*
   Yes _____ No _____

3. *Have an unwavering one-track mind?*
   Yes _____ No _____

4.   *Have a seemingly defiant attitude?*
Yes _____ No _____

5.   *Display strong empathy toward others?*
Yes _____ No _____

6.   *Possess a good sense of humor?*
Yes _____ No _____

7.   *React strongly to guilt or shame-imposed situations?*
Yes _____ No _____

8.   *Often feel misunderstood or unheard?*
Yes _____ No _____

9.   *Get bored easily, especially in school?*
Yes _____ No _____

10. *Refuse to do things that they are told to do without reason?*
Yes _____ No _____

11. *Possess deep and wise-looking eyes?*
Yes _____ No _____

12. *Show strong creativity and talent, perhaps even giftedness?*
Yes _____ No _____

13. *Dislike structured environments such as school?*
Yes _____ No _____

14. *Often behave like they are royalty?*
Yes _____ No _____

15. *React strongly when they are not taken seriously?*
Yes _____ No _____

16. *Get angry when their rights or free choices are not taken into consideration?*
    Yes _____ No _____

17. *Rebel against authority or imposed structure?*
    Yes _____ No _____

18. *Have allergies or reactions to specific foods containing sugar, dyes, and chemicals or to products containing synthetics?*
    Yes _____ No _____

19. *Make profound statements and have a strong interest in God or spiritual concepts?*
    Yes _____ No _____

20. *Have an affinity toward angels, fairies, invisible friends, dolphins, rocks, or crystals?*
    Yes _____ No _____

21. *Grasp concepts and ideas rapidly?*
    Yes _____ No _____

22. *Suffer from depression and/or insomnia?*
    Yes _____ No _____

23. *Have a long memory and rarely forget things?*
    Yes _____ No _____

24. *Have a strong sense of self and identity?*
    Yes _____ No _____

25. *Rebel against ritual-like situations?*
    Yes _____ No _____

26. *Show symptoms of attention deficit disorder (ADD) or attention deficit hyperactivity disorder (ADHD)?*
    Yes _____ No _____

27. *Show alternative or innovative solutions to problems?*
Yes _____ No _____

28. *Call it as he or she sees it when communicating?*
Yes _____ No _____

Is your child:

29. *Very intelligent, even if school grades are low?*
Yes _____ No _____

30. *Often told that he or she is not trying hard enough?*
Yes _____ No _____

31. *Described as a "daydreamer" or "living in fantasy"?*
Yes _____ No _____

32. *Intuitive or does he or she display telepathic or psychic abilities?*
Yes _____ No _____

33. *Intolerant of abusive situations—human, animal, environmental, etc.?*
Yes _____ No _____

34. *Intolerant of deceitful behavior, such as lying?*
Yes _____ No _____

35. *Technologically oriented?*
Yes _____ No _____

36. *A nonconformist?*
Yes _____ No _____

37. *Comfortable being out in nature, around plants and animals?*
Yes _____ No _____

38. *Extremely independent or self-reliant?*
Yes _____ No _____

39. *A loner or likes to work alone?*
    Yes _____ No _____

40. *Not afraid of telling people what he or she thinks or feels?*
    Yes _____ No _____

41. *Emotionally sensitive?*
    Yes _____ No _____

42. *Very sharing and giving, always thinking of others?*
    Yes _____ No _____

43. *Attracted to color and patterns?*
    Yes _____ No _____

44. *Often accused of being difficult or argumentative?*
    Yes _____ No _____

If at least twenty-two answers were "yes," there is a good chance your child may be an Indigo. Your child is most likely Indigo if you answered more than forty questions with a "yes."

Are You Adult Indigo or Indigo/Crystal Cusp?

Note: This questionnaire, although designed for adults, can be adapted for teenagers and older children.

1. *You are intensely passionate about what you believe in.*
    Never _____ Rarely _____ Sometimes _____ Often _____ Always _____

2. *You feel strongly that you have a purpose in your life.*
    Never _____ Rarely _____ Sometimes _____ Often _____ Always _____

3. *You often feel misunderstood when you communicate with others.*
    Never _____ Rarely _____ Sometimes _____ Often _____ Always _____

4. *You are brutally honest with people around you.*
    Never _____ Rarely _____ Sometimes _____ Often _____ Always _____

5. *You have no biases toward sexuality or unstructured relationships.*
    Never _____ Rarely _____ Sometimes _____ Often _____ Always _____

6. *Injustice and ignorance anger you.*
    Never _____ Rarely _____ Sometimes _____ Often _____ Always _____

7. *You can always tell when someone is lying.*
    Never _____ Rarely _____ Sometimes _____ Often _____ Always _____

8. *You have experienced psychic episodes and may even know or sense things before they occur.*
    Never _____ Rarely _____ Sometimes _____ Often _____ Always _____

9. *You are a "straight-shooter" when you communicate, and you call it like you see it.*
    Never _____ Rarely _____ Sometimes _____ Often _____ Always _____

10. *Superficial conversation irritates you greatly.*
    Never _____ Rarely _____ Sometimes _____ Often _____ Always _____

11. *Emotionally, you are loyal in your relationships with people, almost to a fault.*
Never _____ Rarely _____ Sometimes _____ Often _____ Always _____

12. *Spiritual and/or esoteric subjects greatly appeal to you.*
Never _____ Rarely _____ Sometimes _____ Often _____ Always _____

13. *You are a nonconformist.*
Never _____ Rarely _____ Sometimes _____ Often _____ Always _____

14. *You enjoy being with and around people.*
Never _____ Rarely _____ Sometimes _____ Often _____ Always _____

15. *You are best in an occupation where you can work alone and independently.*
Never _____ Rarely _____ Sometimes _____ Often _____ Always _____

16. *You have had profound spiritual experiences such as sensing the presence of angels or deceased loved ones.*
Never _____ Rarely _____ Sometimes _____ Often _____ Always _____

17. *You have a strong desire to help others either individually or globally.*
Never _____ Rarely _____ Sometimes _____ Often _____ Always _____

18. *You get frustrated easily, especially if someone does not understand what you are saying.*
Never _____ Rarely _____ Sometimes _____ Often _____ Always _____

19. *You rebel if someone tells you what to do, especially without explanation.*
Never _____ Rarely _____ Sometimes _____ Often _____ Always _____

20. *Being in and around nature, plants, and/or animals fills you with joy and peace.*
Never _____ Rarely _____ Sometimes _____ Often _____ Always _____

21. *When you communicate with someone, you enjoy keeping strong eye contact with them.*
Never _____ Rarely _____ Sometimes _____ Often _____ Always _____

22. *You resent playing mental or emotional games.*
Never _____ Rarely _____ Sometimes _____ Often _____ Always _____

23. *You always tend to see an alternative side or a different angle to situations.*
Never _____ Rarely _____ Sometimes _____ Often _____ Always _____

24. *You see ideas as three-dimensional or even multidimensional patterns.*
Never _____ Rarely _____ Sometimes _____ Often _____ Always _____

25. *You are highly intelligent, even if your grades weren't tops in school.*
Never _____ Rarely _____ Sometimes _____ Often _____ Always _____

26. *You experience or have experienced depression to varying degrees—ranging from sadness to great despair, perhaps even thoughts of suicide.*
Never _____ Rarely _____ Sometimes _____ Often _____ Always _____

27. *You see the universe as very God- or Creator-centered.*
Never _____ Rarely _____ Sometimes _____ Often _____ Always _____

28. *You are highly aware of what others are feeling or thinking.*
Never _____ Rarely _____ Sometimes _____ Often _____ Always _____

29. *Organized religion does not interest you.*
Never _____ Rarely _____ Sometimes _____ Often _____ Always _____

30. *You have a strong will and a strong temper.*
Never _____ Rarely _____ Sometimes _____ Often _____ Always _____

31. *You are satisfied when you have enough money to cover your basic needs.*
Never _____ Rarely _____ Sometimes _____ Often _____ Always _____

32. *You get angry if your rights or choices are taken from you.*
Never _____ Rarely _____ Sometimes _____ Often _____ Always _____

33. *You often feel distracted, disorganized, restless, and unable to finish things.*
Never _____ Rarely _____ Sometimes _____ Often _____ Always _____

34. *Determination and a dogged persistence are strong characteristics for you.*
    Never _____ Rarely _____ Sometimes _____ Often _____ Always _____

35. *You have sensitivities to a variety of things such as foods, dyes, chemicals, pollution, noise, and synthetic materials.*
    Never _____ Rarely _____ Sometimes _____ Often _____ Always _____

36. *You are strongly attracted to creative endeavors, such as music, art, design, photography, handwork, writing, and spiritual disciplines.*
    Never _____ Rarely _____ Sometimes _____ Often _____ Always _____

37. *You are often introverted.*
    Never _____ Rarely _____ Sometimes _____ Often _____ Always _____

38. *You choose your friends with great care.*
    Never _____ Rarely _____ Sometimes _____ Often _____ Always _____

39. *Sexuality for you is a spiritual connection—creative, expressive, and often inventive.*
    Never _____ Rarely _____ Sometimes _____ Often _____ Always _____

40. *You have a tendency to "think things to death."*
    Never _____ Rarely _____ Sometimes _____ Often _____ Always _____

41. *Guilt-imposed situations have no impact on you.*
    Never _____ Rarely _____ Sometimes _____ Often _____ Always _____

42. *You always try hard to be heard and understood.*
    Never _____ Rarely _____ Sometimes _____ Often _____ Always _____

43. *You have a chameleon-like quality and tend to adapt to situations around you to better connect with people.*
    Never _____ Rarely _____ Sometimes _____ Often _____ Always _____

44. *You prefer an unstructured learning or working environment.*
    Never _____ Rarely _____ Sometimes _____ Often _____ Always _____

45. *You are drawn to the healing arts and/or have a natural ability to heal others.*
   Never _____ Rarely _____ Sometimes _____ Often _____ Always _____

46. *You love working with your hands and constantly creating things.*
   Never _____ Rarely _____ Sometimes _____ Often _____ Always _____

47. *You are very protective of your personal space.*
   Never _____ Rarely _____ Sometimes _____ Often _____ Always _____

48. *You are drawn to crystals, stones, and rocks.*
   Never _____ Rarely _____ Sometimes _____ Often _____ Always _____

49. *Whether you show it or not, you are easily offended.*
   Never _____ Rarely _____ Sometimes _____ Often _____ Always _____

50. *You are drawn to magical concepts such as wizards, fairies, mermaids/men, and unicorns.*
   Never _____ Rarely _____ Sometimes _____ Often _____ Always _____

When you have completed this questionnaire, give yourself the following points:

0 for Never
1 for Rarely
2 for Sometimes
3 for Often
4 for Always

If your score was 176–200:
You are very likely Indigo-Crystal or Cusp. Like all Super Sensitives, you have a purpose and a mission to fulfill. Fully embracing who you are and stepping into your knowing is vital.

If your score was 140–175:
There is a strong possibility that you are indeed an Indigo or shifting into an Indigo-Crystal. You are here with a definite purpose of being a groundbreaker, teacher, and/or messenger. It is important for you to come to terms with and

accept your purpose, and to hurdle some major life challenges. You are like the brave shepherd who will lead the world to water.

If your score was 88–139:
It is possible that you have some Indigo attributes and could be an Indigo forerunner. This means that part of your purpose is to endure some major life challenges and go against the grain to pave the way for future Indigos to arrive. You will become a model for them, a sort of way-shower. You are like the sun urging the young plant to grow tall, reaching for the light that you shine.

If your score was 0-87:
You are not necessarily carrying the Indigo energy, but you are still highly aware, open, and attuned to the world around you. If you are reading this book, it is probable that your life's purpose is closely tied with Indigos, perhaps as a parent or caregiver of an Indigo. This is a demanding role that requires inner strength and understanding. You are like the ground in which the seed will be kept safe and warm as it grows.

Are You Crystal?

Note: This questionnaire can be adapted for both children and older persons.

Do you:

1. *Feel that you are different than other or most people around you?*
    Yes _____ No _____

2. *Have a strong interest in God?*
    Yes _____ No _____

3. *Fairly often make profound or wise statements?*
    Yes _____ No _____

4. *Have a pull toward the outdoors and/or being in nature, whatever the weather?*
    Yes _____ No _____

5. *Gravitate toward being around animals?*
    Yes _____ No _____

6. *Crave time alone and being with yourself?*
    Yes _____ No _____

7. *Prefer communicating without using words, i.e., through thought instead?*
    Yes _____ No _____

8. *Enjoy working and creating with your hands?*
    Yes _____ No _____

9. *Like making crafts or pursuing artistic mediums?*
    Yes _____ No _____

10. *Typically enjoy working in groups or with others?*
    Yes _____ No _____

11. *Get overwhelmed by noise and negative energy such as arguing or yelling?*
Yes _____ No _____

12. *Typically "call it as you see it" when you communicate?*
Yes _____ No _____

13. *Avoid wearing or surrounding yourself with dark colors?*
Yes _____ No _____

14. *Like to collect or work with crystals, stones, or rocks?*
Yes _____ No _____

15. *Have an affinity for multicolors or rainbows in any aspect of your life (clothes, pens, markers, art, etc.)?*
Yes _____ No _____

16. *Get overwhelmed by commotion, pressure, or responsibilities, especially if they come all at once?*
Yes _____ No _____

17. *Get upset when someone tells you what to do and doesn't explain why?*
Yes _____ No _____

18. *Get angry when confronted with guilt or shame-filled statements or situations?*
Yes _____ No _____

19. *Tend to be focused when working on something that interests you?*
Yes _____ No _____

20. *Have an affinity toward veganism or vegetarianism?*
Yes _____ No _____

21. *Find yourself having extremely acute senses: taste, smell, hearing, seeing, feeling?*
Yes _____ No _____

22. *Have sensitivities to food, especially synthetics, additives, dyes, chemicals, and pesticides?*
Yes _____ No _____

23. *Have trouble getting to sleep at night?*
Yes _____ No _____

24. *Consider yourself to be a fearless person?*
Yes _____ No _____

25. *Find yourself getting angry or intolerant when you feel that your freedom or right to choose is being taken from you?*
Yes _____ No _____

26. *See yourself as self-reliant and independent?*
Yes _____ No _____

27. *Usually possess a great sense of humor and a happy disposition?*
Yes _____ No _____

28. *Have a strong need or desire to help others, individually or globally?*
Yes _____ No _____

29. *Have a strong sense of self and know who you are?*
Yes _____ No _____

30. *Often see and show alternative solutions to problems?*
Yes _____ No _____

31. *Have an unwavering one-track mind?*
Yes _____ No _____

32. *Possess deep, intense, and wise-looking eyes?*
Yes _____ No _____

33. *React strongly when you perceive that people are not taking you seriously or are disrespecting you?*
    Yes _____ No _____

Are you:

34. *Emotionally sensitive?*
    Yes _____ No _____

35. *Like a chameleon where you tend to adapt to situations around you to better connect with people?*
    Yes _____ No _____

36. *Extremely intuitive, psychic, or just "know things"?*
    Yes _____ No _____

37. *Telepathic and feel like you can connect with another person's thoughts and feelings?*
    Yes _____ No _____

38. *Often angry when people behave or speak without integrity or do not tell the truth?*
    Yes _____ No _____

39. *A strong person externally, but internally you feel fragile?*
    Yes _____ No _____

40. *Still trying to figure out life and your place in it?*
    Yes _____ No _____

41. *Gifted in any specific area of life: art, music, writing, science, math, technology, etc.*
    Yes _____ No _____

42. *Usually protective or obsessive about your personal space?*
    Yes _____ No _____

Have you or your child:

43. *Been diagnosed as having ADD, ADHD, or autism?*
     Yes _____ No _____

44. *Been told that you are delayed or impaired in your speech or hearing?*
     Yes _____ No _____

If at least twenty-two answers were "yes," there is a good chance you or your child may be a Crystal. You or your child is most likely Crystal if you answered more than thirty-eight questions with a "yes."

The External Hallmarks: Through the Eyes of the Super Sensitive

CHAPTER NINE

Children are the bridge to heaven.[9]

—Persian Proverb

Perhaps you've seen them or even have some yourself. They can be happy, highly sensitive, and sometimes temperamental. They can even be seen as difficult. Yet, when you look into their eyes, you know that they are special—wise old souls in small bodies. When they speak, many speak a special language, saying profound and wise things. These are the waves of children being born today on this planet—children that are born pure in spirit. They are truly a new breed, unlike anything seen on a large scale in previous generations. These children are the Super Sensitive: Indigos, Crystals, and Indigo-Crystals or Cusps. If you are reading this book, you either are one or are a parent or guardian of one or you heard about them and are curious.

Even though the distinctive essence of the Super Sensitive relates to their unique vibration or soul color, it is important to look at the external hallmarks. In our human lives, we are governed mainly by the five senses—seeing, hearing, feeling, tasting, and touching. Our understanding of the world is intimately tied to those senses. The outward characteristics of the Super Sensitive vary and are distinctive. To have a better understanding of them and know how they (and perhaps you) fit within this world, we need to look at the physical, spiritual, and emotional characteristics, the behaviors, and the responses through the eyes of Indigos and Crystals. And we need to see how they relate to our current human timeline.

Parts III and IV will give an in-depth explanation of many of those characteristics from the Indigo-Crystal perspective, from personal experience and knowledge. You'll also learn strategies and tips that caregivers and educators can use to help young children cope and successfully survive.

Indigos

Indigos have inhabited this planet since the dawn of time. Indigos have come in sporadically, some unnoticed and some very noticed and labeled as misunderstood or different. From about 1945 onward, small numbers of Indigo children were being born. Many arrived after 1985. I was born before 1985. My vibration is described as Indigo-Crystal, because I resonate to Indigo and Crystal energy and light and have characteristics of both, much like being on an astrological zodiac cusp, hence the term Cusp.

The term "Indigo children" is a generality. While society is much more conscious of Indigo children who have entered this life within the last decade or so, many Indigos in this century are not children per se. They are teenagers, adolescents, and adults of all ages. If you bristle at the thought of being called a child and know that you are Indigo, keep in mind that this term is being used because of the mass consciousness awakening to the Indigo concept.

Being Indigo is very much a process, and many people who have come in with varying blended rays or vibrations of Indigo, such as Violet/Indigo or Blue/Indigo, have shifted and evolved energetically over time. I came in as Indigo and gradually through much of my own personal healing and energetic work evolved more into Crystalline vibration.

But not every person runs Indigo energy, blended or otherwise. If you or your child was born after 1992, it is very likely that you, he, or she is an Indigo. *The reason?* Our planetary evolution is about shifting our vibration. Take a look around you. Change is occurring faster and faster: the earth is in chaos; many situations are tumultuous; and awareness of global connections is growing rapidly. That means our own personal frequencies and vibrations are increasing rapidly as well.

As we evolve into higher awareness, we shift along the color spectrum. Therefore, more and more children being born will be heading toward the Crystalline end of the spectrum and less of every other color. In short, that means that with every Indigo and Crystal child born, the consciousness of the planet rises.

The percentage of Indigos arriving has increased within the last decade to where I believe that the vast majority of children being born now are Indigos, perhaps up to 99 percent. Within this next decade, the large numbers of new Indigos will peter out, primarily because their personal missions are either fully under way or complete, making way for more Crystal children and higher consciousness to come through. If you were born before 1992, does this mean that you are not an Indigo? Absolutely not! There are Indigos born every year, but in the past, the percentages were not as high.

Lately, there has been a lot of information on the Internet about the differentiation of the waves of Indigos according to the decade they came in. I even briefly differentiate the different waves in my next book, *The Psychic Indigo: Guide to Spirit Connection.* Each of these "waves" is classed according to a specific time frame. For example, the First Wave arrived post-World War II, Second Wave in the late 1960s, and so on. And depending on which wave you were in, your personal or global mission was different, as well as your characteristics. Some people claim that these early waves were not Indigos at all, or weren't "pure" ones.

Let's put a halt to this thinking right now. In terms of your purpose to help raise consciousness, it doesn't matter overall whether you as an Indigo were born in 1967 and were in the Second Wave, like me, or were born in the 1980s in the Third Wave. Society is inundated with labels, and we certainly do not need more of them. The key here is to simply *be* the Indigo, Crystal, or Cusp that you are. Being it supersedes the human need for classification. Everyone has a mission. Everyone is here for a reason. When you came, it was correct and perfect for you to be here. All that matters is to recognize yourself and why you are here, embrace it, and get on with it.

The main reason why generalized timelines are used to identify when the Indigo vibration increased is because in earlier eras it was harder to ascertain their presence. Sometimes, though, they stood out and had such an impact that they were described as "quirky," "genius," or even "heretic." Indigos of the past include Joan of Arc, Albert Einstein, Saint Bernadette, Wolfgang Amadeus Mozart, and Vincent Van Gogh, to name a few.

Indigos are also "lightworkers." Lightworkers are souls who came here to spread light and love, to elevate consciousness, and to help heal the planet from fear. Indigos are here to make a difference in this world. They have multilevel purposes: one level is personal, the other global.

The movies *Indigo—The Movie!* and *The Indigo Evolution* helped introduce the world to the presence of Indigos among us. The movie and the documentary are about a seemingly "normal" child who exhibits strikingly unusual characteristics and behaviors. Books about Indigos include *The Indigo Children* and *An Indigo Celebration*, both by Lee Carroll and Jan Tober, and *The Care and Feeding of Indigo Children* by Doreen Virtue.

So, media aside, how can we identify the Indigos more concretely? As a parent, teacher, or caregiver, your first inkling is your sense that a child is "different," though you may not be able to pinpoint what the difference is. There are numerous characteristics of Indigos. Here are the distinctive features relating to the physical, emotional, behavioral, communication, response, spiritual, and purpose levels.

Indigos:

- Are very sensitive to the environment (can include foods and additives), energy fields, and electrical currents, as well as emotional sensitivity to what is happening around them.

- Often are great multitaskers, accomplishing many things within a short time and having many projects going at once, but not necessarily following through on all of them.

- Can display extreme physical, autoimmune or energetic issues such as chronic fatigue syndrome, fibromyalgia, lupus, extreme mania, or freneticism.

- Have difficulties focusing unless it is something they are fully interested in, and then their focus is 100 percent. Otherwise, they fidget and can't sit still.

- Often feel depressed, suffer from extreme sadness or hopelessness, battle insomnia, or have suicidal feelings or thoughts.

- Have a strong tendency to feel misunderstood. Social settings in school are challenging.

- Can show the full spectrum of emotional expression, from crying to stoicism.

- Are strong willed and have a determination that is sometimes described as "warrior-like."

- Can suddenly become fiery tempered. Usually the temper comes forward when there is injustice or misunderstanding; when they are on a mission; or when other people's words and actions are out of alignment, and they are determined to expose it.

- Will often do the exact opposite of what they are told.

- Get easily frustrated, especially when asked or told to do something without being given a reason or purpose. Being told to do something "because I said so" does not work.

- Possess good senses of humor.

- Are bright and intelligent, though they may not earn great grades in the mainstream educational system.

- Will often "call it as they see it" and won't hold back from doing so. They are blunt and straightforward and sometimes labeled as "tactless."

- State what they want or need very clearly.

- Can be technologically oriented. They usually are whizzes at computers and other gadgetry.

- Can be diagnosed or misdiagnosed as ADD, ADHD or ODD.

- Are usually self-reliant.

- Do not respond to or buy into to guilt or any shame-filled situations. They see right through this game.

- Are often introverted or are loners. They seem antisocial unless they meet others like them; then they suddenly change.

- Are nonconformist and rebel against structure and authority. Very often they come up with innovative ways of solving problems.

- Can run into trouble with specific systems they see as outdated or ineffectual—systems such as legal, educational, political, personal, or medical.

- Are usually rebellious in school and in other mainstream institutions or structures.

- Feel "different." They often behave like royalty.

- Are intolerant of deceitful behavior and will call the person on it.

- Have built-in lie detectors. They have the ability to see through illusions. They can tell when someone is lying or dishonest, or out of integrity with their words, thoughts and behavior.

- Are intolerant of situations that do not allow for their free will or choices to shine through. Decisions made for them are usually unacceptable.

- Have no tolerance for abuse of any kind—human, animal, or environmental.

- Have little tolerance for what they perceive as stupid behavior.

- Question everything. They always want to know the reason or basis for a question or statement.

- Love being around plants, animals, water, and anything outdoors.

- Have a deep empathy for people, animals, and all living things.

- Are highly intuitive and can be telepathic and show extrasensory capabilities, communicating with spirits, angels, fairies, or other "invisible" beings.

- Make profound statements and have a strong interest in God. They seem wise beyond their years.

- Have an affinity for much color or specific colors; they often reject dark colors.

- Are gifted in one or more areas, such as music, math, science, technology, art, and drama.

- Are highly artistic and creative and enjoy making things with their hands.

- Have a strong need to help others, individually and globally.

- Know that they are different and feel as if they don't belong on Earth or fit in society.

- Seek out relationships based on strong soul connection rather than just physical attraction.

- Have no prejudice against any type of sexuality.

- Will search for a deeper meaning to life and try to find their place in the world.

- Know that they are different and don't necessarily know how to fit in.

It is important to know, though, that regardless of how differently they demonstrate it, these children come into this world by choice. They know that they have an inner agenda. By demonstrating their differences through their speech, thought, and behavior, they assist us in breaking old paradigms of perception and overall ways of being. The Indigos are the new generation of superheroes that help expand the consciousness and evolution of this world.

Crystals

Just when you thought you were getting used to the idea of the Indigos—the not-so-new kids—there is another group of "new" kids that is rapidly populating our planet. The next waves are the followers of the Indigos, dubbed the Crystal children for their crystalline soul colors, energy patterns, and iridescent personalities. The majority of the Crystal children that are here now have come after the mid-1990s. Some are children of older Indigos. There are some Crystal adults, but most adults with crystalline traits are Cusp or Indigo-Crystal.

Like Indigos, Crystal children—or Crystals—are here for a purpose: to follow the trailblazing path of the Indigos toward a safer and more secure world. While Indigos are the warriors and the leaders who chop down everything in their paths that smacks of old structure and paradigm, Crystals are here to usher in harmony. They are the peacemakers and healers; the ones who will provide innovative solutions and perspectives in a harmonious and loving manner. One example is the now well-known British chef Jamie Oliver, why is on a mission to change the way people and schools think about feeding children. To date, he has taken on more than fifty-five schools and helped change the school lunch habits for more than twenty thousand children in the United Kingdom.

The characteristics of Crystals overlap with those of Indigos, but there are some differentiating traits.

Crystals:

- Know that they are different.

- Are telepathic and/or extremely intuitive.

- Are very bright, intelligent, and mentally astute.

- Have an affinity for multicolors or rainbow colors.

- See and/or talk to angels, spirits, people that have crossed over into spirit, and "invisible" beings.

- Are drawn to magical concepts or entities, such as fairies, unicorns, mermaids/men, and wizards.

- Have a strong interest in God and make profound or wise statements.

- Love to wear mismatched clothes.

- Gravitate toward light or bright-colored clothing and usually reject dark colors unless paired with bright colors.

- Have skin that is easily irritated by such things as clothing tags or seams.

- Love taking off their clothes, especially young children. Diapers and clothes feel cumbersome, and they love being naked. Getting Crystal babies and young children to stay dressed is often a challenge.

- Love crystals, stones, or rocks and things that sparkle.

- Love to hug or touch others, spontaneously or otherwise.

- Love to collect things from the outdoors, such as crystals, rocks, and leaves.

- Are comfortable around plants and animals.

- Have an affinity for the outdoors and nature. Rain or shine, they will be outdoors.

- Love being in water and enjoy anything associated with it.

- Have an affinity for dolphins, whales, and other gentle, water-oriented animals.

- Have acute senses of smell and taste.

- Are sensitive to a multitude of things, such as foods, additives, pesticides, chemicals, pollution, dirt, electricity, noise, and vaccines. Their emotions also may be sensitive.

- Can get overwhelmed by pressure, responsibilities, and commotion.

- Can be protective of their personal space.

- Have great empathy toward others' feelings and needs.

- Have an inherent ability to uncover people's fears. They connect with people's heads and hearts.

- Are developed in their "clairs"—clairvoyant, clairaudient, clairsentient, claircognizant. They can see people's energy especially when words and actions are out of alignment.

- Possess natural healing abilities.

- Are usually fearless.

- Love to stay awake.

- Must have an explanation when asked to do something; doing something without reason never works.

- Are intolerant of situations that do not allow for free will or choice. Decisions cannot be made for them.

- May be vegan or vegetarian.

- Like to keep their rooms or spaces neatly organized.

- Can be very focused. They do not like to stop a project once they have started it.

- Can work cooperatively in groups, especially when there is mutual respect.

- Like to work alone.

- Are independent and self-reliant.

- Are artistic, creative, and gifted in one or more areas, such as art, music, math, science, dance, writing, and acting.

- Are hand-oriented; they like to build or create things.

- Can be technologically oriented, adept with computers and other gadgets.

- Do not like being confined in small spaces, including the womb.

- Sometimes can behave like a bull in a china shop; not particularly graceful.

- Will "call it as they see it" and will not hold back from doing so.

- Can be perceived as defiant and strong-willed.

- Will do the opposite of what you tell them to do.

- Will suddenly shake and move their bodies around, especially in circles—clockwise and counterclockwise.

- Are very clear on what they know and what they want and will communicate it bluntly.

- Do not respond to guilt or shame-filled situations.

- Are nonconformists.

- Will cry or get angry, but the emotions will release as quickly as they flared up.

- Often have large, clear eyes that look as if they are staring right through you.

- Have an external fragility or sense of vulnerability yet are strong internally when focused and determined.

- Have great senses of humor.

- Are usually happy and in good spirits.

- Have gentle, compassionate, and forgiving personalities.

- Can be delayed in speech and may be diagnosed as having impaired hearing or speaking.

- Can be labeled as having ADD, ADHD, or autism.

- Have a strong need to help others, individually and globally.

- Are not concerned about whether they fit in or not.

Unlike Indigos, Crystals come into this life not afraid of showing that who they are is normal and not something unusual. I recently came across a program on *The Oprah Winfrey Show* that featured children with extraordinary abilities in many areas of life. One segment featured a young Crystal artist who was able to paint what looked like a masterpiece in only thirty short minutes. While the audience and Oprah sat astounded by this seemingly miraculous feat, it was clear to me that was the typical Crystal child ability. This was normal to Crystal children but considered extraordinary by most others. To them, what they demonstrate is no big deal; to many others at this time it is.

As with all people, Super Sensitives come into human life as perfection but enter a seemingly imperfect world. There is often a great disparity between the energy of their inner higher wisdom and that of this world in its current consciousness. The difficulty this brings is twofold. Many Super Sensitives do not have a full conscious understanding of how to fit in a world that does not necessarily support them at this time in its evolution. Also parents, guardians, teachers, and friends do not know how to counsel and guide them through these rough waters.

Now It Makes Sense to Me!

So you've taken the quiz, either for yourself, your child, or someone you know. You've probably discovered whether or not you resonate to the Indigo or Crystal energy. If you resonate to the Indigo energy, wonderful! One way to recognize this is through an inner resonance that vibrates within you. Your resonance is something that strongly impacts the deeper part of yourself. It's almost like winning the lottery—that first feeling of surprise, the giddiness that follows, and then the feeling of jumping for joy. Only this time, that joy pervades throughout you, perhaps creating a feeling of "Aha, now I get it."

I have received many e-mails and communication from people who say their moment of recognition feels like a lightbulb turning on inside of them. Many have reported a feeling of coming to a place where the confusion of not fitting in or not belonging finally made sense to them. However, awareness is only halfway to the destination. And the destination is about being an Indigo or Crystal in the world and living in full consciousness of who you really are. The trick now is figuring out how to *be* an Indigo or Crystal in this rapidly changing world.

So now that you've reached the recognition stage and come down, albeit slightly, from the high of knowing with every cell in your body that you are Indigo or Crystal, where do you go from here?

Uniqueness exists all around us. While a rose can be instantly identified, there are a multitude of varieties, each with their own characteristics and beauty. Each human being carries a unique stamp of energy known by our fingerprints. There are no two alike. Even identical twins have their own unique fingerprint. In that uniqueness lies the sum total of our potential, what we have discovered and yet to discover about ourselves.

Take the sculptor with a slab of marble. On the exterior, all you see is a stone. But to the creative mind, there is potential for something grand, and it is just waiting to be born. The sculptor is simply the instrument by which that dormant potential is awakened into something that is full of life and demonstrates purpose.

The nineteenth century philosopher Henry David Thoreau said:

"What lies before us and what lies behind us are small matters compared to what lies within us. And when we bring what is within out into the world, miracles happen."[10]

Once you recognize that you are definitely Indigo or Crystal, it is a matter of you assuming the role of the sculptor, taking the next steps, and integrating that resonate knowing within you to figure out how to create that which is waiting to spring forward.

Each of us has some sort of talent or skill. We are all born with accessibility to the universal pot of talents and skills. There is a good chance that something dominant showed itself early in childhood. Perhaps it was artistic ability, communication or expression, teaching, writing, or perhaps something more of a global nature. Equally weighted with our talents and skills, lie the challenges along the path of life—adventure, adversity, difficulty, and fears along the way. Each challenge can be viewed as the key to unlocking a door. And behind each door lies a treasure—a lesson, an opportunity for learning, growth, and expansion. Each treasure is designed to help us discover life's purpose and express it.

That is what being Indigo or Crystal is all about: discovering the uniqueness and transcending the challenges. Transcending is also about the pieces of the puzzle finally coming into place, seeing the whole picture, and having a full understanding of it before coming into actualization. But first, one must unlock all those doors, each with its own special key, to get there.

SO, I'M AN INDIGO— NOW WHAT?
The 25 Keys to Survival
PART III

Know Thyself

CHAPTER TEN

What do you seek, O Pilgrim on the Path?
"Liberation from pain and freedom from all suffering."
The answer to thy quest is already in thy heart.
Listen, O Pilgrim, to the whispering of thy Soul…
"Know thyself…for in thyself is found ALL there is to be known.[11]

—from the Records of Wisdom

"Know Thyself." Isn't it interesting that an Indigo's ultimate key to survival dates as far back as the sixth century BC, coming from an ancient maxim purportedly inscribed over the Temple of Apollo at the Oracle at Delphi in Greece? "Know Thyself" made its way to ancient philosophers such as Socrates and Plato and has continued on to this day. It is a concept that strikes at the very core of every human, whether they were aware of it or not. This simple phrase means learning how to be who you are and being conscious of, understanding, and living *everything* that is contained in who you are as an individual. In other words, it is all about the good, the illusory bad, *and* the ugly.

Knowing oneself is a fabulous first step. The second, and probably the more crucial, is to know how to get along and coexist with all the other "selves" that reside on the planet. The latter is like learning to be a parent. There is no one-size-fits-all solution. And there is no owner's manual.

When I was growing up, people often told me to be myself. I thought it was simple. All I had to do to be liked, accepted, respected, approved of, admired, and anything else that fell into the general societal acceptance category was to "be myself." Everything that involved a connection to others was about being "me."

The tricky question was just exactly what was that? *What did it mean to be myself? How could I be myself, if I didn't know myself?* And probably most important was that once I "knew myself," how did that make any difference in my life?

My journey for the first thirty-three years was about exactly that—discovering and knowing myself. What I uncovered, however, was that it was the discovery process that led to the knowing, which was the key to survival of this Indigo. Undergoing the process was what made the difference, because it pointed to a crucial piece of the puzzle that all Indigos face—the purpose for being here, which is to serve the world in a global way.

First, you need bring the real you out into your consciousness. Here are some strategies and concepts toward uncovering that.

Key #1: Know That You Are Here by Choice

Yes, it's true. You are here on this planet by your own choice. Let that sink in for a minute, or two, or three. Let me repeat this. You are here on this planet by *your own choice.* You chose and, might I add, volunteered to be here. When did you make this choice? Before you came here—that is, before you incarnated into this body in which you reside.

Your soul is infinite, unlimited, and all-knowing. Your human body is merely a vehicle your soul operates to have a variety of experiences and to use its infinite knowledge in numerous ways. You could say that your soul, or spirit, is truly who you are. The rest of you—this body that you have chosen—is allowing you to humanly express all that you are as spirit. And it is your spirit that holds all the answers.

But...*I don't remember making this choice,* you say. To some degree that's true. When we incarnated into human form, we decided to temporarily cover up our knowledge of who we really were. The way to remember is to go through many experiences that aid us in bringing that inner knowledge back to light. It is like wearing Harry Potter's cloak of invisibility inside out. Essentially, we make ourselves invisible to our true selves and go through the human journey to discover new ways to express our inner selves visibly.

You choose many of the experiences you go through as a human being. Each of us designed our life plan. It's like creating a life blueprint. Before our incarnation, we fleshed out the basic plan. We chose our parents, siblings, the type of life to be born into, location of birth, gender, relationships, how long we would live, how and when we would depart this life, lessons to learn, specific people to help us learn those lessons quickly, types of experiences that help us best learn those lessons, the purpose or mission that we needed to fulfill, and a basic theme that could either be something challenging to overcome and/or a way that our purpose would be expressed. My description of our so-called destiny is that we design a skeletal plan before incarnation, but we flesh it out through our free will—our individual choices that we make on a microsecond-by-microsecond basis while in our human bodies.

Even though you may have gone through part of your life wondering why you've had chaos, crises, upheaval, misunderstandings, confusion, and other problems, you are not a victim of your circumstances. You have chosen every aspect of your life. Your soul knows who *it* is, and it knows who you are and why you are here. It's a matter of tapping into it and not ignoring it.

Key #2: Determine Your Values

Because you are here by choice, what is valuable to you will undoubtedly show itself in your life. One of the tricks to surviving as an Indigo in this world is to understand what is important to you. Knowing your values is vital to defining who you are and figuring out what you stand for. Your values are your personal inventory of what you deem to be important and what is of interest in your life. They help give your life meaning.

For example, when I was twenty-five my declared value was that I wanted to help heal people. Years earlier, when I was in fourth grade, I had undergone a career and personality test. The results suggested that a career in the counseling, healing, medical, artistic, or writing fields would be most suitable for me. Even though I paid little attention to it then, ironically, that's exactly what I ended up doing. But the discovery process was important. I uncovered my values through my feelings. If they promoted joy and peace, and energized me, then it was a clue to unraveling my values. I discovered that I valued things like altruism, creativity, helping others, honesty, integrity, ethics, respect, leadership, spirituality, mind-body-spirit connection, and especially that we had full power to choose how our lives were designed and lived.

You need to dig inside yourself and determine what is important to you. One way to do that is to ask yourself how you feel about certain things. For example, if you hear the words "helping others," what is your first feeling? Does the energy feel uplifting or does it drag you down? Your feelings are your inner guidance system and provide clues to who you are. They never let you down. So use them—constantly.

Key #3: Determine Your Personal Operating System

Guess what, Indigo? You have come with your own unique set of beliefs, concepts, values, and views. The frustrating part is that how you see things seems different from many people around you.

You are here to help break the existing belief structures, especially ones that are already perceived as being broken or dysfunctional. Yes, you and many others like you are here to do that. The reason why your paradigms, beliefs, or viewpoints don't fit in is because they are not supposed to. We did not choose to come here to blend or fit in. Trying to do so will only frustrate you.

It took me a while to realize that I was doing my spirit a disservice by trying to ignore my paradigm. I spent many years trying to express what my beliefs were in the face of a system that didn't fit mine. One day it struck me that the system that I operated from was not going away. In ignoring it, I wasn't honoring that part of myself. Spending countless years stomping your inner feet and wondering why you don't fit is fruitless, so let yourself off the hook.

Consider your paradigm as your personal operating system, just like that of a computer. Your paradigm is a conglomeration of your assumptions, concepts, values, and practices. It takes your view of the external world and determines how you internalize it. It takes your internal memory and experiences and determines how to express them to the external world. Figuring out your operating system—the basic design from which you work—is the key to knowing yourself.

You can start by asking yourself some provocative questions such as these.

- What do I believe about religion and spirituality?
- How do I feel about gender equality? Human rights?
- How do I feel about abuse of humans or animals?
- What do I believe about war, chaos, or fighting?
- How do I feel about God?
- What abilities do I have in this life?
- What do I believe about myself?
- What are my strengths?

- What do I value?
- What are my passions? What "lights my fire"?

You get the drift. Once again, let your feelings rule. They will let you know through their energizing quality which aspects are part of your paradigm.

Key #4: Connect with Others of Like Mind

This step is one of the more accelerating ones to undertake. Surrounding yourself with others who have either engaged in similar thinking, viewing, or working helps you to build a better understanding of who you are.

The world in 2006 is waking up. Lightworkers span the globe. We are jam-packed with healers, energy workers, educators, and more. When I was growing up, there was nothing around that gave me the impression that there was anybody else like me. Basically, the consciousness of the planet had not been raised enough to allow for this. That was pre-Internet. Thankfully, the Internet has connected us all around the globe.

Now, there are many organizations and groups that cater to Indigos, Crystals, and the broad category of Super Sensitive. I refer to some of them in the resources section. For connection and support, I have a group set up for Indigos and Crystals on Yahoo Groups. It is important to connect with others, whether through specialty-related groups such as healing circles, support groups, personal development workshops, energy groups, and study groups, or through general get-togethers. It is the conscious connection that gets you out of your sense of isolation and the belief that you are alone. You aren't!

You Have a Purpose

CHAPTER ELEVEN

For each soul enters with a mission... We all have a mission to perform... Why did I come into the earth at this time? That it may be bettered by thy service... That's the purpose of each soul.[12]

—Edgar Cayce
Twentieth century psychic and visionary

Everyone on this planet, past, present, or future, has a purpose. It is impossible not to have one. After all, we don't just hang out on this Earth for nothing, whiling away the time until we leave it. Without exception, everyone has a personal growth mission. Whether it is learning about patience, forgiveness, compassion, or love, just to name a few, we all have some theme that is pervasive throughout our lives. Discovering that theme helps us to know ourselves, which directly leads to our own individual soul growth and expansion.

It's like going to college and picking a major and a minor course of study. Every one of us does this before our incarnation. On the soul level, this is the predetermined portion of our lives—predetermined by us. We chose the themes, and that is why no matter what path we walk once we are here on Earth, we cannot leave this life until we connect and fulfill our theme that we have chosen.

Indigos take that one step further. Not only do they have their own personal growth to undergo, but they all have a calling to serve. In other words, Indigos have multilevel themes.

126

This is one of the distinguishing features of an Indigo. Service is the name of the game. The calling for Indigos, often one of a global nature, usually shows itself early in life. What that means is that the nature of their service will somehow affect a large number of people.

When she was six, my Crystal daughter, Katerina, displayed the beginnings of her global service by writing stories about children, dolphins, angels, and fairies. She has continued to write stories, and now, at age ten, plans to write a book.

My calling is to serve and reach many people quickly with information and awareness, a calling that led to this book. My theme as a writer showed itself as early as age five, when I sat at that typewriter in kindergarten and proclaimed that I was writing a book. It never ceased. For a while I ran from it, especially from the structures imposed on me through educational systems telling me how to write, when to write, and what to write about. There was a time when I abhorred writing and stopped completely, afraid of words and afraid that I would have nothing to say. I bought in to the inner critic who told me that I had no voice and that you had to be famous to write anything worthwhile. But the more I ignored the quiet, still feeling, the more it came back to find me, until one day I understood that this theme wasn't going away.

I had temporarily forgotten that I had chosen this theme, and I was doing my soul a disservice by not facing it. The more I ignored it, the more I felt depressed, tired, and anxious. A whole set of aches and pains increased the farther I steered from my purpose. I had to face the fact that my purpose lay in writing. When I realized that I had chosen this, and therefore I was the only one accountable if I didn't embrace it, the feeling of letting myself down was enough incentive for me to step fully into my purpose.

Herein lies the challenge—discovering the purpose, figuring out how to channel that purpose into the world, and demonstrating the purpose in the face of controversy, adversity, or opposition. Let's face it—it's hard out there in our society. We live in a society that's plagued with systems, structures, and huge expectations on how to be, live, think, and do. For an Indigo with a global purpose, determining how to discover and know oneself and then place that purpose into action amidst contrary societal expectations is a challenge, especially for younger Indigos.

I believe that a person's second most important question in life is to ask themselves why they are here on this planet. For a great many of us, it is not apparent, especially early in life. But throughout our lives, as we experience many situations, we grow and learn, and, in short, we evolve. It is like being on a roller coaster. You don't get on the roller coaster just to get to the end of the ride. You experience the ride for the thrill of it. It is the same with being Indigo. It is about the process. Discovering why you are here and what you are here to do *lies purely in the process.*

The good news about process and evolution is that the process includes stages: awakening to it and then moving into purposeful action. Where you are going may not be apparent right now, but this is the part where you get to flesh out the intricate details through conscious choices that you make daily.

Your purpose and reasons for being here unfold over time, and you have much to contribute. Your purpose is the responsibility that you have to contribute to others. Finding what your purpose is centers on around your gifts. While there may be many, many moments of frustration, especially since your purpose may be not apparent, know that you need to hang in there. The Indigo process is like the bulb in the ground: You may not see the flower yet, but growth is taking place where you can't see it.

So how do you figure out what you are here to do? Once again, it's about looking within. The next four keys can help you determine your purpose.

Key #5: Use the Gifts with Which You Were Born

You are unique in that you bring your individual gifts to this planet through your birth. The gifts are your natural talents—characteristics that you chose to express in this lifetime that were evident from the get-go. These are the abilities that came naturally to you. You had no formal training—you were just good at them. For example, your physical abilities, your personality, your looks, the way you communicate or think, an ability to easily play a musical instrument.

If you are an adult or an Indigo youth right now, take a moment to think back to your childhood:

- What were you naturally good at?
- What came easily to you without any thought whatsoever?
- What did you enjoy?
- What did you love to do?
- What did you tell yourself that you wanted to do?
- What did you dream of doing before other people's opinions got in the way?

Now zoom forward into the present and look at your life. Ask yourself the following questions:

- If you were to teach someone something, what could you or would you want to teach?
- What would you say are your unique abilities?
- If you asked someone to tell you what you are an expert on, what would they say?
- What do you feel passionate about? (These can be joyful feelings or feelings of anger that compel you to action.)

The answers to these questions will give you clues as to where your purpose lies.

Key #6: Take Stock of Your Strengths and Interests

Now that you've figured out what you are naturally good at and can do without much thought, take a survey of what your interests are. The clues are scattered all over the place. Again, your feelings can help you determine what place these will have in your life.

My interests as a child stretched from music to reading and writing. However, to refine that, what I loved to read, watch on television, or talk about was people's life stories, their personal struggles and challenges, their journeys and experiences, and their triumphs. When I watched television programs, what drew my attention were characters who were internally powerful, fearless in their voice, willing to stand up for the underdog, and ready to challenge anything that lacked integrity. In my childhood fantasy, I wanted to be like those people. As an adult, my interests in those areas shifted from watching television to writing and becoming like those characters, just in a different way. In other words, my interests came from relatively positive experiences that I chose to develop, refine, and master. This book, among other things, is a reflection of those strengths and interests.

Life is a journey above all. During that journey, everyone occasionally gets caught up with life and tends to overlook their interests or strengths. When that happens, the signs usually rear their heads, letting us know that we've become too caught up with the little details of living, and not being in our purpose. Questions you can use to take stock of where your strengths and interests lie are:

- What were your favorite things to do in the past? In the present?
- What kinds of books do you like to read?
- What types of conversation stimulate you?
- What activities make you lose track of time?
- Who or what inspires you?

Key #7: Fall in Love with What Is in Your Heart

Lebanese poet and author Kahlil Gibran had tremendous insight when he said, "When you are born, your work is placed in your heart."[13]

Your heart is your feeling place. Your passions running through your heart and soul are based on feeling. When you are passionate about something, it brings an energizing feeling, like the freedom of a bird soaring through the sky.

Your purpose has the same quality to it. It is filled with a feeling of overwhelming joy and passion. You can be passionate about many things. Does that mean everything you are passionate about is your purpose? No. For example, I can be passionate about being a superstar basketball player, but if I'm only five feet tall and have no athletic abilities whatsoever, then it is certainly not my purpose. Even if I chose to devote 100 percent of my energy to that passion, it wouldn't net me a spot with the Chicago Bulls. It would also leave me very broke and starving, because my energy would be going out toward this passion but getting me nothing in return.

So, even though there are many things we can feel passionate about, there is usually one major thing that would make us get out of bed every morning. That's the feeling of falling in love. When you uncover it, you can't help but feel like you are in love with your life 24/7. You can't think of anything but that, and when you shift into that mode, life becomes meaningful and expansive.

Remember when you fell in love for the first time? Remember that sense of giddiness and excitement, the feeling like you were on cloud nine and nothing could bring you down? Many people make fun of this state and seen it as unrealistic. But that is our true state of being. The bliss state is very real. And shifting into purpose is exactly like that. It is *very* real, and it is continuous.

Passion, however, is like a coin. It has two faces. One is the passion of love. The other is another strong emotion—usually anger. This refers not to anger that makes you want to hurt someone, but rather an anger toward something that you believe is wrong or violates someone's rights. It is the type of anger that fuels action toward something positive, standing up for something. Perhaps it's something you see on television or behavior around you. Perhaps it's a belief that you carry inside of you that just knows that a certain way of behaving or acting is wrong. But whatever it is, it is passionate, and it's there inside of you for a reason, waiting to come forward. So examine both sides. Ask yourself these self-examination questions:

- What excites you about people?
- What excites you about the world around you?
- What do you see or hear about that angers you?
- What global or personal issues get you angry—angry enough to do something or speak up about?
- What cause would you stand up for and vocalize your support for?
- What are you passionate enough about to speak out on?
- What message would you bring to people if you could do that?

An example of an Indigo's passion in action is British chef Jamie Oliver. His passion and medium is food. His mission is global—breaking apart an old paradigm of how children are fed in schools. He has set out to change the entire school lunch program to promote healthy and balanced eating, eliminating junk and other unhealthy food.

Passion often stems from feeling very emotional about something. Sometimes you trigger your passion through challenges, hurdles, or negative experiences. This book is a result of the challenges I faced and the negative experiences I hurdled. Without those challenges, I wouldn't have been able to write this. Instead of choosing to be a victim or blaming my circumstances, I chose to channel the passion into something purposeful. In the process I discovered that my purpose was to help others discover theirs.

Key #8: Resistance to Your Purpose is Like a Boomerang—It Always Comes Back

The clues to our purpose are always there. Sometimes we run away from them. But as the saying goes, "What we resist persists." It comes back in your face over and over again, until you look at it.

It took me until the age of thirty to really get that "Writer" was my theme—that I had chosen no less. While the Universe gave me a reprieve I'm sure while I was growing up, the theme showed up more and more as I got older. Eventually, the episodes were so intense and obvious that I couldn't ignore them. I finally surrendered to them.

A wise person once told me that the bigger the fear you experience, the bigger the purpose that you have. Think about what you fear the most right now. Is it speaking in public? Writing? Voicing an important issue? Sharing your story? Whatever it is that makes you want to sink your head in the sand like an ostrich is a big clue for you. And the Universe is unconditionally loving and offers unlimited opportunities for learning. The more you run away from your purpose, which may what you most fear, the more often it will keep showing up. And it doesn't matter how old you are, it will still keep showing up until you get it. Remember, the Universe gives you unlimited chances.

So don't run away from your purpose, regardless of your inner critical voice or what others say or think. Be courageous—be the warrior that you are.

Mastering the Emotional Roller Coaster

CHAPTER TWELVE

This being human is a guest house. Every morning there's a new arrival—a joy, a depression, a meanness. Some momentary awareness comes as an unexpected visitor. Welcome and entertain them all. Even if they are a crowd of sorrows who violently sweep your house empty of its comforts. Still, treat each guest honorably. He may be cleaning you out for some new delight. The dark thought, the shame, the malice. Meet them at the door laughing and invite them in. Be grateful for whoever comes, because each has been sent as a guide from beyond.[14]

—Rumi
Sufi poet and mystic

We are blessed with many things in our lives, and there is one vital "something" that we all have when we come into this world, Indigos included. We *all* have the capacity to feel. We arrive as feeling beings. Feeling is part of our natural state, which is pure love.

Our human bodies are vehicles—vehicles into which our spirits get expressed in a unique, individual form. Pierre Teilhard de Chardin, a Jesuit priest in the early 1900s, put it well when he said:

"We are not human beings having a spiritual experience, but rather spiritual beings having a human experience."[15]

To understand your emotions the spiritual way, think about a science experiment on light refraction. When you take white light and shine it onto a prism, the light refracts. What you see is the light spectrum broken into the colors of the visible part of the spectrum. Feelings are like the visible light spectrum. The prism is our human form. The white light is our true state—love. When we channel the pure state through our humanness, it allows us to feel everything on the spectrum— joy, anger, frustration, anxiety, depression, and all the other emotions.

While human beings tend not to feel more than mixed emotions some sporadically, Indigos carry feelings to the next level. They feel everything—all the time. Life to an Indigo is experienced through feeling. Indigos cannot disassociate from their feelings. They feel what they feel, whether it's tuning to people and feeling their emotions, feeling nature, feeling for animals, or feeling the chaos around the globe. Imagine a feeling as a radio station. While most of us tune into one station at a time, an Indigo feels like the dial is tuned to a hundred radio stations at once and with the volume cranked up. Feelings are tied to intuition and being tuned in with the greater knowing of the spirit or soul.

Sometimes an Indigo's level of feeling is so deep that it is difficult to get through it, especially when the feeling is pain, despair, depression, anger, or anxiety.

Key #9: Experience the Dark Night of the Soul

The roller coaster of emotions is part of the process of being Indigo. Going through the gamut of feelings and emotions is part of the process that ultimately leads to full awakening of who you really are, why you are here, and how you are meant to express your purpose in life. The challenge lies in dealing with that gamut while being in the middle of it. Feeling all the feelings can be a downright ugly experience, but it is necessary to the survival of the Indigo.

An Indigo's life is full of phases. While many of us arrive on this planet with lots of intuition, full of gifts, and plenty of knowing and awareness, the fact that Indigos feel different is usually the hardest feeling to handle. Many of us don't know why we feel different, just that we are. Trying to make sense of all that is challenging, because we can't escape the feeling—it's part of us.

So here's the deal. The first major phase of awakening to your Indigo-ness is a passage. It's like a ship moving through a channel during the night before entering open sea in the daytime. I call it the Indigo's Dark Night of the Soul.

Being an adult or adolescent Indigo is like being a late bloomer. And going through the dark of the night of the Indigo soul is no picnic. The time when one awakens to their full self is different for everyone. There is no right time, chronologically or otherwise, other than when you chose it to be. I woke up fully at thirty-three. However, I can say that even though my dark night of the soul lasted until about twenty-five years of age, between then and my awakening, it was clear that the clouds were dissipating on the horizon, signaling the end of my passage. But everyone is different—and yet everyone has to experience it. There is no escape.

During your dark night, you as an Indigo probably experienced great chaos. Perhaps you chose to be in a family or relationship that seemed difficult or dysfunctional. Perhaps you felt no sense of belonging. Maybe you wondered what on earth you were doing here. Perhaps you were in an environment where the educational system seemed in opposition to what you knew to be right inside. Maybe you felt anger toward injustices that you noticed around you and felt helpless at not being able to do something. Or perhaps you just felt different and misunderstood. Every time you tried to communicate what you felt or observed, you were knocked down or ignored.

Whatever the challenges, it was necessary to experience every feeling associated with them. You are not only feeling your own multilevels of pain, frustration, anger, fear, apathy, hopelessness, and anxiety, but you are tuning in to other people's feelings as well, individually and globally. Experiencing the feelings and going through this rough period is preparation for your true purpose to shine through and be put into action. Remember, your purpose is one of leadership. The bottom line of a leader is that you cannot help someone and be of service unless you have "been there, done that," and can share what you did to survive and come out the other side. So you need to go through it, because out of it comes strength and a unique perspective that can be channeled into a purpose—to serve the world.

Key #10: Ditch the Sword: Become the Spiritual Warrior

One of the main hallmarks of an Indigo is having a warrior spirit. Being a warrior conjures up images of battle, anger, passion, drive, courage, focus, and fearlessness. Indigos are often described as angry warriors. *But angry at what?* Usually injustice in its many forms—abuse, lack of integrity, and so on.

During the wake-up phase of my life, I did a lot of clearing and healing work on myself. I worked on healing the physical self, which was growing daily in pain and discomfort, and the emotional self. I wanted to get to the bottom of why I had always felt angry.

Whenever I experienced bodywork, it was customary for me to receive visual or emotional information, especially from my spirit guides or angels. Flashes of pictures, messages, or specific bits of feelings would come to mind as I was receiving acupressure or massage, for example. During one of these times I uncovered what I believe to be the roots of the Indigo's anger.

What I received was the message that Indigos went far back in history, as far as ancient Lemurian and Atlantean civilizations. Indigos had roots stemming from Lemuria, which was primarily a race of peace and harmony. Indigos were land-based people, and communication was telepathic—through thought energy. In other words, their natural state was one of being intuitive. There was respect and honor for all people, nature, and animals, and there was knowledge that everything was connected. Through time, as beings migrated around the globe, that peaceful civilization became disrupted.

As new people settled among the Lemurian population, they brought in different ways of being and behaving. Gradually, telepathic communication broke down, and lack of respect for the land and the people in it took over. Over time, one's natural state—intuition—was buried, as words and physical communication and behavior took over. The new inhabitants became more aggressive in their ways of speaking and behaving. Abuse and struggle for power moved in.

The Indigo people were forced to move and migrate to other parts of the world. Their anger rose as they watched the destruction and abuse of the land that was once peaceful and harmonious. They became angry at people displaying violent and aggressive behavior. They became angry at people not living in their integrity—saying one thing, but acting differently. Anger grew as they watched people disconnect from their spirits and lose touch with who they were. When people disconnected from their spirits, words, which carried a lower vibration, were often out of alignment with intentions, motivations, and actions. The anger and frustration has remained in the memory of DNA and been carried forward into the present through the current Indigos.

This planet is evolving rapidly. Awareness of people around the globe is increasing. World events such as natural disasters like earthquakes and tsunamis and violent destructive wars are calling people to reach deep inside of themselves and connect with their spirit.

Part of an Indigo's purpose is to help bring back peace and harmony to this planet. However, the strong emotional memory embedded in the DNA shows itself early on in an Indigo's life. This intense emotion is two-sided: When an Indigo displays bursts of anger or rage, it can be disturbing to those around, but paradoxically, it can also be the impetus toward great change.

The Indigo process includes experiencing these intense warrior-like emotions. It's like using a machete to chop down something that stands in the way of reaching their goals. But to survive these emotions and fulfill your purpose (and by the way, you will), the Indigo needs to shift from angry, machete-chopping warrior to peaceful or spiritual warrior. Why?

Well, here's the deal with anger. Anger is one heck of a powerful emotion. It is also very destructive, especially when fear lies beneath it. Anger and other powerful emotions are nothing more than reactions to external situations. That means that there usually are a multitude of events or experiences that "push your buttons" and lead to feelings of anger.

The frustration of the Indigos lies in the round-and-round reactions to life's challenges—injustice, abuse, destruction, violence, disrespect, and more. Because you, the Indigo, are trying to figure out your place in the world, absolving yourself of the anger that gets triggered is an important key to your survival.

So what's the secret? Well, Indigos are natural warriors; that part will never change. It is the energetic suit of clothes we came with. However, it is important for warriors to be discerning and pick their battles; to do so, they tune in to their higher knowledge that rests within them. That's what you have carried with you into this life. You just need to use it—to get through your process and survive it. Turning inward is key. Turn to the ultimate source of love that is your true state. Only then do you become the Spiritual Warrior and able to step fully into your purpose.

So what does the Spiritual Warrior look like?

Spiritual Warriors:

- Come from a place of love and compassion.
- Have discovered their inner spirits and know who they are.
- Are attuned to themselves as human beings.
- Know their purpose.

- Carry themselves with integrity.
- Feel the fear but don't let it stop them from taking action.
- Accept and love the dark parts of themselves.
- Forge ahead despite obstacles and challenges.
- Embrace the connection with all things in the Universe.
- Do not focus on the past or the future, only the present.
- Accept their intuition as part of who they are.
- Are disconnected from the drama of life.
- Put their egos on pause to listen to their spirits.
- Come from their place of inner power.
- Are courageous without needing to start a war.

So Indigo, let go of reacting out of anger. Dump the sword. It isn't the sword that's going to help you survive or get through this any faster. Reacting in anger to other people's choices of action and behavior isn't the solution. Lashing out in anger all the time is counterproductive to your purpose. One cannot usher in peace, harmony, and balance to this planet through anger. It can only be done by tapping in to the higher, all-knowing part of you that is removed from reaction.

Start observing what is happening around you as if you were watching a movie. Replace your anger with persistence and insistence. You alone have the power to choose how you will emotionally respond to what is going on. You have total control over your emotional roller coaster. By getting off the roller coaster, you step into a higher, more expansive level of awareness that allows you to see higher lessons in every situation that presents itself.

Key #11: Let Go of the Past and Feel the Feelings Fully

One of the keys to survival is to not live in the past or perceive yourself as a victim of life. Many Indigos during their searching phase are confused and frustrated. There is a tendency to feel like a victim.

Remember, you are here by choice. Before your incarnation, you volunteered to be here. Earth is going through a major shift in energy and changing rapidly. From a soul point of view, this is an exciting time; we are changing for the better. Rather than sitting back in spirit and watching it all happen, you volunteered to be here in the middle of it, to help facilitate the change. How courageous of you! You wanted to be in the thick of things—to help turn this planet into a world of peace, not war.

Letting go of whatever is in your past is vital; otherwise it will keep you there and stop you from forging ahead in your purpose. Instead of blaming others or your circumstances for how you feel, accept your feelings for what they are, no more, no less, and without judgment or attachment.

Allow yourself to feel everything to its fullest extent. When you utilize your capacity to feel fully, how you respond to situations will change and become more effective. So do not avoid the feeling. This leads me to the final key of this lesson.

Key #12: Escape Mechanisms are not Coping Mechanisms

Many Indigos, especially teenagers or young adults, going through the rough passage *do* experience the deep gamut of emotions. Because of the intensity, both of their own emotions and from tapping into other people's emotions, it can be a heavy burden. This phase is tenuous, as it is tempting to want to escape from feeling the emotions fully. The desire is often to resist feeling, because the feelings are so intense and overwhelming. We tell ourselves that we don't want to feel so much, so there is a temptation to turn to escape mechanisms—drugs, alcohol, or thoughts of suicide or bodily mutilation. For those considering such an escape—don't!

There are many safe and constructive coping mechanisms for dealing with intense emotions. Harm in any form isn't one of them. Replace your urge to grab for pain-relieving or emotion-numbing substances with something non-destructive. Take a nap, go for a walk, work on a hobby, move your physical body, play a sport, engage in meditation, talk to a friend, breathe—the list could go on and on. Always choose a nondestructive route to get through the feeling.

The next chapter will further explore specific energy management techniques.

Energy Management

CHAPTER THIRTEEN

Meditation brings wisdom; lack of mediation leaves ignorance. Know well what leads you forward and what holds you back, and choose the path that leads to wisdom.[16]

—Hindu Prince Gautama Siddhartha
founder of Buddhism

When I was growing up, I saw everything as energy around me. I would often find myself slipping into a mesmerized state while staring at people or things around me. I didn't know anything about energy fields or that we all had one, but I knew what I saw. I just couldn't understand it and, more importantly, I couldn't understand what I could or should do with it.

We are all energy and vibration. You. Your car. The trees around you. The desk that you work on. The chair that you sit on. The ground that you walk on. The key that you press on the piano. The music that you play. Your pet dog. Your body. Your emotional self. And especially your thoughts, words, actions, behaviors, feelings, and beliefs. Everything is energy and vibration. There isn't one thing that is *not*.

Indigos come in understanding this and consciously recognizing that they are aware of energy in many ways. Whether it is your intuition, clairvoyance, clairaudience, sensing, feeling, or describing it simply "his vibes were off" or "I just knew that," these are all ways of plugging into and utilizing energy. Most often Indigos feel like they are at the mercy of the energy. They experience it randomly or sporadically, and feel as if they have no control over it. To survive, you need to learn to manage energy—because you can. There are some basic things you need to know about your Indigo energy system.

Key #13: You Feel Different Because You Are!

Let's talk about basics for a minute. You are energy, and you inherently know it. You have come into this life, knowing that you are somehow different. You feel it, but perhaps you can't figure out why. The reason is simple—your energy is different. There is a difference in your energetic template—your auras and chakras.

Everybody has sensed an aura at some point. How many times have you stood in front of a person and either you or they backed off slightly, leaving a certain amount of space between you? This is because of the aura or energy field that surrounds each of you, defining your personal space. So whether or not you are consciously aware of feeling an energy field, you are nevertheless recognizing it on some level.

Consider meeting a person for the first time. You know the expression that first impressions are everything? Well, the first impression that you pick up is that other person's energy field. If what you pick up is slightly "off," and you feel that something is not quite right with this person, that is usually an indication that the person's energy field is uneven or out of balance, or perhaps that the nature of the person's thoughts and feelings does not quite match with what is shown on the surface. These experiences are based on energy fields.

Your aura is the electromagnetic field that surrounds, penetrates, and emanates from all beings and living things. It has many layers, some stretching as far as twenty feet in all directions. Different colors are associated with many parts or layers of the aura—technology such as Kirlian photography has captured auras on film. Layers of the aura are associated with different vibrations, with each layer carrying information about the person.

While the aura is considered very broadband, your chakras within the auric field are concentrated energy centers that co-relate with the surrounding layers of the aura. "Chakra" is a Sanskrit word, describing swirling, cone-shaped vortices that run along the energy field of the spinal cord in the human body, usually up and down. This flow of energy from the base of the spine is called kundalini energy.

There are thousands of chakra points throughout the body, but the traditional chakra template has seven main energy centers from the base of the spinal cord to the top of the head or crown. Each chakra relates to emotional, mental, physical, and spiritual aspects in addition to carrying specific colors, sound frequencies, and elements as follows:

The Third-Dimensional Chakra System and Template

No.	Chakra	Location	Color	Note	Element
7th	Crown	Crown	Purple-White	B	Cosmos
6th	Third Eye	Mid-Brow	Indigo-Violet	A	Light
5th	Throat	Throat	Blue	G	Ether
4th	Heart	Heart	Green/Pink	F	Air
3rd	Solar Plexus	Solar Plexus	Yellow	E	Fire
2nd	Sacral-Spleen	Navel	Orange	D	Water
1st	Root	Tailbone	Red	C	Earth

The chakra system of Indigos, Crystals, and Cusps is very different. The auric bodies or layers of energy are expanded, more refined, and more developed. As all information is held in the energy field, Indigos therefore carry and are more consciously plugged into the Universal database of knowledge. That's why you tend to just "know things" without necessarily knowing how you know. You just know— period. By being plugged in to more conscious thought, your energy centers, through which information and knowledge flow, are expanded and awakened.

The Indigo chakra template is considered to be the Fourth-Dimensional Chakra System and is comprised of at least thirteen chakras. For brevity, the Fourth-Dimensional Reference is about moving beyond duality, polarity, and our three-dimensional way of life. In essence it is about tapping into the concepts of quantum physics. While there are more than thirteen chakras, for simplification, the current system cuts off at thirteen.

The Fourth-Dimensional (Indigo-Crystal) Chakra System/Template

No.	Chakra	Location	Color
13th	God Self	2 feet out from Heart	Rainbow/White Gold
12th	Ascension	22 feet above Head	Rainbow
11th	Multidimensional	15 feet above Head	Rainbow

No.	Chakra	Location	Color
10th	Divine Creation	8 feet above Head	Magenta/Gold
9th	Christ Soul	4 feet above Head	Gold/Silver
8th	Divine Love	Whole Head/Crown	Violet/White
7th	Heart	Chest	Violet/Pink/Red center
6th	Left/Right Hands	Palms of L/R Hands	Violet
5th	Root/Spleen	Lower Abdomen	Red/Orange
4th	Left/Right Hips	Hips	Orange
3rd	Left/Right Knees	Left/Right knees	Green/Orange
2nd	Left/Right Foot	Soles of L/R Feet	Yellow/Green
1st	Earth Star	2 feet below Tailbone	Rainbow/Platinum Silver

The 13-Chakra System overview:

Chakras 1–5
Lower Chakras—Connected with the physical body and the Earth.

Chakras 6–7
Heart and Hands—Connected with soul love and healing from the heart; expression of divine love through a physical way.

Chakra 8
Divine Love—Our expression of the divine knowing, spiritual compassion and awareness, astral travel, and karmic patterns, residue, and cleanups.

Chakra 9
Christ Consciousness—Our connection to Christ and our soul blueprint; all our information about our soul through all lifetimes and beginning of existence resides here.

Chakra 10
Divine Creation—Our experience with synchronicity, blending of masculine/feminine energy; manifestation of thoughts into form; works in conjunction with chakras 6 and 7 for physical expression.

Chakra 11
Multidimensional—Recognition of your self as existing in no time and in all spaces simultaneously; this is the main concept behind quantum leap, teleportation, bilocation, and telekinesis.

Chakra 12
Ascension—Total connection to the Universe and oneness of everything; this includes God, Christ, angels, archangels, ascended masters, and reciprocal communication.

Chakra 13
Unconditional Love/God Self "the god in me sees the god in you"—True joy, bliss, and our interconnectedness with the divine or God; seeing ourselves as energetic extensions of God. This chakra extends about two feet out from the heart and is indicative of expression of unconditional or divine love from one's heart and soul.

The kundalini energy that flows through the chakras in the third-dimensional, seven-chakra system typically moves in an upward direction starting at the base of the spine. In popular meditative exercises, the energy movement is depicted by visualizing earth energy coming up from the ground and divine energy flowing down through the crown chakra to blend and meet in the middle.

The Indigo/Crystal energy system moves differently. Energy flows down through the upper five chakras (nine through thirteen), down through the head and heart, through the spine down to the base of the spine (fifth chakra). At the base of the spine, the energy turns and moves back up the spine and outward. As it moves outward, the energy creates a large oval circle moving out past the arms and down, all the way to the feet, and then finally back up again through the base of the spine to the thirteenth chakra. If you were to visualize this as a more solid picture, you would most likely see the energy creating a winglike shape, similar to an angel. In chapter 14, you will read about techniques for connecting with and harnessing the energies of the upper spiritual chakras.

Unlike the third-dimensional chakra system, the chakras of the Indigo-Crystals arrive fully open and activated. This explains why many children come into this world fully exhibiting the "clairs," healing abilities, or artistic gifts, as well as having profound thoughts and alternative viewpoints.

Having this template is a gift—a gift that Indigo-Crystals bring to the rest of the world. Their expanded chakra system fully opens them to their purpose, consciously or not. Because their purpose is to usher in peace and harmony, they bring a gift of expanded awareness through their energy system as an opportunity for the rest of humanity to follow and expand into—if they so choose.

Key #14: Become Intimate with Your Energy

Part of being Indigo is becoming aware of your own energy. Because your chakras are activated, open, and operating at practically full speed, it is important to learn what your energy feels like, so you can best know how to manage it.

One of the quickest and most basic ways to feel your energy is through your hands. To simply feel your own energy, rub your hands together as quickly as possible. You will be creating friction between your palms. If you feel heat, this is your energy. Now move your palms away from each other slightly, several inches apart. Bring them in slowly and then pull them back out again. Do this several times. Notice the magnetic push and pull that has been created between your palms. Now play with your energy. Lay your hands on a person, or a plant, or on yourself. Notice what happens, what it feels like, or what responses you get.

Okay, that was a simple warm-up. Let's increase the pace. Let's start to visualize our energy to see how far it extends and what it feels like on a greater scale. Visualization is the art of creating mental images. You may sit or stand for this exercise.

1. If you are sitting, sit back in your chair comfortably.

2. Uncross your legs and allow yourself to feel your spine relax against the back of your chair. If you are standing, stand with your legs slightly apart, arms hanging loosely by your sides.

3. Start by relaxing your muscles one by one, starting from the soles of your feet, working your way up your legs, thighs, and pelvis (feel your pelvis and the base of your spine settle into the chair). Continue up through your torso, chest, fingers, arms, and shoulders. Finally, work your way up the head and feel the tension drain from your scalp.

4. When you feel you are relaxed, visualize a ball of golden white light emanating from the center of your being.

5.   See this light grow larger and expand outward from your center, until it is past your body and is surrounding you.

6.   Visualize this energy surrounding you like a bubble.

7.   Play with this energy bubble. Notice what it feels like. Does it have an edge? How far does it extend? Does it have color? What is the texture of the energy? Do you notice anything else that may be unique?

8.   When you have completed this, bring your awareness back to your body and the sounds around you.

9.   Get up, stretch, and move around.

That was a basic centering and exploring exercise. Centering is a powerful technique, especially with sensitive Indigos whose energy can easily be thrown off-balance due to the expanded chakras. Taking the time to center yourself several times a day is a good approach to managing your energy. This will help ground you and assist you in becoming more solid in everyday life interactions.

Key #15: Ground Yourself

As an Indigo, your energies are usually wide open and vulnerable. Being vulnerable means your energy so wide open that practically anyone could walk right in and meddle with it. This is called psychic polluting or attacking.

When we utilize our "clair" abilities, we are tapping into the upper chakras and downloading information and knowing. When we interact with people in any way, our energies tend to intermingle. In other words, your consciousness touches everyone else's consciousness. Imagine having one radio station turned on and playing, while simultaneously bringing in several more. Confusion would result. The more sensitive you are, the easier it is for you to be affected in many ways—emotionally, physically, mentally, and spiritually.

Part of being sensitive means taking responsibility and managing your energy, so that you do not allow yourself to be affected by other people's energy that bombards you from all around. Once you are more aware of the way your energy feels, the next step is to ground it and become solid in it.

To understand what being grounded feels like, let's look at its opposite. Ungrounded usually refers to the soul being out of body or not in touch with the physical self. You can experience being ungrounded by:

- Not being fully in the present, but instead living in the past or future.
- Feeling spacey or flighty.
- Feeling frustrated, angry, or short-tempered.
- Excessively worrying or fretting.
- Reacting spontaneously.
- Continuously being distracted.
- Feeling "out of body."
- Habitually tripping over your feet or bumping into the furniture.
- Experiencing difficulty concentrating.
- Getting easily distracted during conversations or jumping around from topic to topic.

From an energetic perspective, to function fully and survive as spiritual beings in physical bodies, it is important to balance the spiritual and the physical. Remember, your purpose is being here in your physical body and anchoring points of light onto this planet. Fulfilling your purpose means you have to be fully present in the physical body, while simultaneously maintaining a high level of energetic vibration. How do you do this? There are many ways of grounding, but here are few quick and basic approaches that are highly effective.

Hug a Tree
This is an oldie but goodie, and yet many of us do not take the time to do this. This is free and easy and takes but a minute.

1. Go out into nature.

2. Find yourself a tree in a forest, park, or close to where you live.

3. Connect with the trees around you. Tune in their energies. You will never pick the wrong tree.

4. When you feel that you have made a connection, allow yourself to touch the tree—feel the bark, the texture, the solidness.

5.   When you ready, wrap your arms around it, place your hands on the trunk, sit on the ground either hugging the tree or with your back to it. You can even climb the tree if you so desire.

6.   Whichever way works for you, allow yourself to blend in with the tree's energy. Feel yourself become one with the tree.

Touch the Ground

This is self-explanatory. Bend down. Place your hands on the ground. Feel the energy and vibration running through your hands and into your body. Repeat as often as desired.

Visualize Your Earth Connection

Stand with your arms hanging loosely at your sides or sit in a comfortable chair with your legs and feet uncrossed.

1.   Relax your body—your limbs, your muscles, your spine—feel yourself sinking downward with your tailbone pressing into the chair.

2.   Allow any random thoughts to pass through. Don't focus on them but simply acknowledge that they are there and put them aside to be returned to later.

3.   Bring your attention to your breath. Take a deep breath in through your nose and exhale through your mouth, letting out all the air from your lungs.

4.   Inhale slowly, counting 1-2-3-4, and hold 1-2-3-4.

5.   Exhale slowly, counting 1-2-3-4, and hold 1-2-3-4.

6.   Repeat this three more times—inhale, hold, exhale, hold.

7.   Now bring into your attention a beam of white light streaming down from your upper chakras, starting at least twelve feet above your head, beaming down through your head, and connecting with your heart.

8.   Inhale the white energy into each chakra, slowing filling them up.

9. Visualize this energy flowing through you, down your spine, out your arms, down through your legs, and through the soles of your feet.

10. See this white energy all around you now, streaming through your whole body, coming out below you, and through your feet.

11. This energy is reaching deep into the earth, like roots from a tree, intertwining with the Earth's core, connecting with all living things—the water, nature, animals, and people.

12. Draw the energy of the Earth back up through the roots, breathing and bringing in rainbow energy—the energy of unconditional love.

13. Feel the pulsing of the rainbow energy moving through your whole body and surrounding you in beautiful, loving, multicolored light.

14. Sit in this energy and feel your connection to the Earth.

15. You may find that the colors change and shift. Whatever color arises for you is necessary for healing at this time.

16. When you are ready, bring yourself back to the present and into your body, and bring your attention to the sounds around you.

Key #16: Set Boundaries and Practice Detachment

Boundaries are distinctive lines that define you as separate from other people. That is not the same as saying that in the grand view of the Universe you are somehow separated or disconnected from others. Universally, we are all one. We are all interconnected. However, from an energetic perspective, we are individualized in our own ways. Setting boundaries as Super Sensitive individuals is important for two reasons: protection and containment.

To learn to draw boundaries, let's define how your energetic self works. Super Sensitives are intuiting, feeling beings, first and foremost. The way we intuit and feel, however, comes in all shapes and sizes. In my experience with hundreds of clients and students, I have come across several groups of energetic distinctions. See if you fit into one of these:

Absorber. The energetic sponge, you absorb other people's emotions or thoughts, to where you can feel drained, anxious, depressed, tired, irritated, or overwhelmed. This commonly occurs in external situations, like walking into a mall or being in a crowd.

Catalyst-Activator. You find yourself drawn to situations where there is chaos or upheaval, or where a person or situation is shifting or changing. After the shift, it is no longer necessary for you to be in that situation. Energetically, however, you must endure the upheaval temporarily, which can leave you exhausted and drained. I fall into this category. It took me a number of years to learn about shielding and protection, so I could be a catalyst without being emotionally involved.

Sensor. You intuit through your senses—hearing, seeing, feeling, smelling, touching. You often sense potential negative experiences or events such as accidents or disasters. When you describe something you will often start with the phrase "I sense...."

Empath: You pick up emotions, thoughts, pain, or conditions about other people and feel them bodily within yourself, often in tandem with the person who is experiencing them in the moment.

Whichever category you resonate to—maybe one, maybe all—it is vital that you set boundaries about how you will control your energy. Practice detaching yourself from situations around you. Become the observer *of* the movie instead of being a participant *in* the movie.

How do you draw that boundary and become detached? There are two main ways:

1.   **Do not give in to the emotional pull that you feel.** Here is where your practice of being grounded comes in. Use it when faced with an emotional or intense situation. The better grounded you are, the less chance you will be pulled in energetically by the energies of others. It takes focus and practice to improve on this. And remember, what other people are acting out, reacting to, responding to, or emoting about are their own feelings, not yours. Even if they are referring to you or talking about you, their feelings, reactions, or responses are still theirs. Practice this affirmation: "*I observe.*"

2.   **If you find yourself absorbing the energy, release it quickly.** The better you are at grounding and keeping your energy protected (see Key

#18), the better you will be at not absorbing energy. Nevertheless, all energy systems weaken temporarily, and at times we end up absorbing unconsciously rather than consciously keeping a firm boundary. Be sure to release anything that is not yours quickly (see Mental Clearing Exercise, Key #20). The key here is to recognize when energy does not belong to you. The more intimate you are with your energy and the way it feels and operates, the easier it will be to discern what energy belongs to another person and to insulate yourself from unwanted energy. Practice this affirmation: "*I now release from my energy that which does not belong to me.*"

Key #17: Create Your Personal Filtering System—Energetic Self-Defense

Energetic protection is important. The reality is that you, the Indigo, are a Super Sensitive being. You hear, feel, see, and intuit practically everything. Whether it's picking up on other people's energy or feeling someone's pain through your body, you understand that you are connected to all things. Because Indigos all truly care about the world, you have a strong awareness about this world and are highly capable of tuning in to practically everything that surrounds you.

Super Sensitives need a strong filtering system. Your aura or energy field is already a natural defense mechanism. This sea of consciousness is always at work. And strengthening it is necessary for survival in this world.

A filtering system allows you to be in charge of your own energy. It enables you to control and filter out the barrage of emotional, mental, psychic, and energetic stimulation and stresses that we deal with daily. It sets boundaries that allow you to keep out unwanted energy, cutting down on the possibility of being overwhelmed. A strong system helps you differentiate your own energy and emotions from those of others. A self-defense system also helps you strengthen your energy while at the same time allowing you to exist and navigate your way through this life.

Over the years of teaching intuitive development and working with Indigos and Super Sensitives, I have come across many techniques on energy protection. Ultimately, I have developed my own, based on channeled information during my workshops. Over a decade ago, the angels who guided me and my teachings supplied me with an energy strengthening method, aptly called the Crystalline Protection Technique. It works extremely effectively with Indigos and Crystals and is very popular with young children. I talk about angels, connecting with deceased loved ones, and psychic development in *The Psychic Indigo*.

The Crystalline Protection Technique

1. Begin by sitting down or standing comfortably, feet flat on the floor, legs and feet uncrossed, arms loosely at your sides.

2. Relax your body one part at a time.

3. Breathe in white light through the top of your head and bring it into your body, into your heart.

4. Breathe in the light, counting 1-2-3-4 as you inhale.

5. Hold the breath, continuing to visualize the light, counting 1-2-3-4.

6. Exhale the breath through your mouth, counting 1-2-3-4.

7. Visualize a bright, ruby-red, heart-shaped crystal centered directly in *your* heart.

8. Breathe in this ruby-red energy, counting 1-2-3-4.

9. As you breathe in, see this crystal expand past your heart, moving through your entire body until it has encompassed you and is surrounding your whole body.

10. Hold the energy, counting 1-2-3-4.

11. Exhale the red energy, counting 1-2-3-4.

12. As you exhale, intentionally anchor this visual, so that you feel the ruby-red energy firmly around you.

13. Take note of how this crystal feels to you. Note its shape, size, and texture. *This is your core spiritual shield.*

14. When you feel comfortable with this crystal shield, visualize a circular, pink quartz crystal also embedded within your heart.

15. Breathe in the pink energy, inhaling and counting 1-2-3-4.

16. Hold the energy of the pink quartz, counting 1-2-3-4.

17. Exhale slowly as you mentally count 1-2-3-4.

18. As you exhale, see this pink quartz expanding and emanating from your heart, surrounding your body, and expanding farther than the ruby-red energy.

19. Play with this pink quartz layer. *This is your emotional shield.* This layer is now larger in radius than the ruby. Make a note of how this feels.

20. When your emotional shield feels anchored, continue to visualize yet another crystal, this time a clear quartz crystal, again firmly embedded in your heart.

21. Breathe in the clear, crystalline energy, inhaling and counting 1-2-3-4.

22. Hold the energy of the clear quartz, counting 1-2-3-4.

23. Exhale slowly as you mentally count 1-2-3-4.

24. Allow the quartz crystal to expand in radius until it surpasses both the ruby and pink quartz layers. *This layer is your mental shield.*

25. Sit with the clear quartz energy, becoming familiar with the way it feels and looks.

26. You now have three crystalline layers around you, each nested within the other.

27. Now visualize a prism rainbow pyramid firmly present in your heart center.

28. Inhale the rainbow energy through your nostrils with mouth closed, counting 1-2-3-4.

29. Hold the energy while counting 1-2-3-4.

30. Exhale the energy through your mouth, counting 1-2-3-4.

31. As you exhale, beam out the rainbow energy in front of you. See it moving out, then up and out, and around your entire body and all the crystalline layers. *This is your outer physical shield.*

32. Sit with this shield of crystalline protection. Feel it sealed off and contained. Become familiar with it—its strength, size, shape, and texture. Adjust your visuals if you feel the needs strengthening in any form.

You have now effectively protected your energy. Remember, you have total control of your energetic shield. Think of it as having a semipermeable property. You have total control what you let in and what you give out.

Your shield will deplete or weaken over time, so you must regularly maintain your shield. Once in the morning when you wake up and once at night before bed are good times to check in on the status of your shield.

Healing and Honoring Your Spirit
CHAPTER FOURTEEN

Spirit is the essence of who you truly are. Listening to spirit is listening to who you truly are and what you are trying to tell yourself. Speaking to spirit is allowing who you truly are to communicate with you and help guide you in this human experience. Feeling your spirit is allowing yourself to feel what you truly are made of. Going against these three things would be doing your spirit a great disservice.[17]

—Olena Gill, from *The Enlightenment Box*

You, Indigo, are a wise old soul. By old, I mean that you carry much eternal knowledge and awareness within you, accumulated from lifetimes of living and existing. Deep down, you already know this. It is evident in the way you feel when you look at people and situations around you. You know things that many don't seem to. You get upset and stamp your inner feet when people "don't get it," don't you? You see spirits, talk with dead people, hear voices, see angels, and many other experiences like that, but you don't talk about it due to fear of how others may perceive you. Or perhaps you wonder if you are crazy? You hide who you really are until suddenly you find others like you, and surprise, out of your shell you come. You also feel angry, lonely, misunderstood, unappreciated, and disrespected, especially for your infinite knowledge that you bring forward and try to communicate.

Does this ring a bell? It should. It's the pattern of spiritual expression that Indigos bring into this human life. Why is that?

155

The Super Sensitives come into life knowing their own perfection. Many are consciously aware, and others are in various waking stages. However, they quickly realize by looking at life around them that it doesn't match or resonate to the truth of who they already know themselves to be. The external world doesn't reflect their inner perfection. It is the stark realization of this disparity that Indigos come to know early in life. This results in feeling depressed, frustrated, angry, and disappointed, and even blocking the voice of your spirit to try and cope. There is pain in your spirit, but to survive and function in this life, that pattern is one that needs to be addressed and healed. You won't be able to fully and confidently put your purpose into action unless this happens. The healing rests purely on the spiritual level.

There are a few issues around spiritual healing and honoring your spirit connection that need to be looked at: recognizing and accepting yourself as a intuitive being; letting go of the pattern language in which you are immersed; and trusting your intuition, so that you can step into your true self with confidence.

Key #18: Intuition Is the Language of Spirit

I just know. I don't know how I know, I just know. I hear voices, sometimes like whispers. I see dead people. I feel things all the time. I sense something is going to happen.

These are just some of the many statements that Indigos make during their process of waking up to their true selves and purpose. Those are statements of intuition. Sometimes called *"the sixth sense,"* intuition is the language of your spirit. It is one of the major ways that your spirit communicates with you about everything, including your connection to the universe.

Think of yourself as part of a gigantic communication system, like the Internet. As a powerful transmitter and receiver through the psychic Internet, information flows in and out of you. Your spirit and those of everyone else transmit and receive, not through words, but through at least four streams of psychic expression. These are extensions of intuition known as the four "clairs." "Clair" simply means *clear* or something *with clarity*. Let us look at the basics:

Clairvoyance

An extension of our physical sight, clairvoyance means *"to see with clarity,"* beyond our physical eyes. Clairvoyance includes spiritual visions, dreams, imagination, and auric seeing. Clairvoyance utilizes the third-eye chakra under the seven-chakra system. Indigos and Crystals use the upper four chakras to receive their clairvoyant information. The positive affirmation for this clair is, "I see clearly."

Clairaudience

An extension of our physical hearing, clairaudience means *"to hear with clarity,"* beyond our physical ears. Clairaudience includes hearing spirit voices, music, and thought telepathy, as well as comprehending spiritual laws. The positive affirmation for this clair is, "I hear clearly."

Clairsentience

An extension of our physical touch, clairsentience means *"to sense with clarity,"* beyond our five physical senses. Clairsentience includes phenomena like empathy (sensing or feeling in the physical body), psychometry (receiving an impression by touching a physical object), and healing. The positive affirmation for this clair is, "I feel clearly."

Claircognizance

An extension of feeling, claircognizance means *"to know with clarity,"* beyond the physical feeling. This is the stream that is being utilized when you proclaim, "I just know." Claircognizance is used in conjunction with the other three "clairs" through all upper chakras of the Indigo-Crystal thirteen-chakra system. The positive affirmation for this clair is, "I know clearly."

Clairaroma and Clairgustus

These are much less popular terms. Clairaroma is an extension of physical smell, and clairgustus is an extension of physical taste.

Every person has a dominant "clair." You probably know what that is, just by your experiences of intuitive reception. Whether it is hearing voices, seeing pictures in your mind, or feelings within your body, there is always one strong stream that comes first whenever you tune into your intuitive space.

Does that mean that if you are mainly clairvoyant, you cannot be clairaudient? No! It is possible to develop all four clairs and become balanced in the way you receive intuitive information.

When I was a young child, my main stream of information came through my knowing. My vision and hearing tied for second place, my feeling came a close fourth, and clairaroma and clairgustus ran a distant fifth and sixth. As I grew older and my intuitive understanding matured, I discovered that my vision strengthened and often shifted into dominance. My dominant form of receiving changed with the circumstances; my psychic sense became chameleon-like.

Getting used to how your intuition comes through and harnessing it so that you can control how streams of information come through is important in gaining confidence, and, ultimately, knowing yourself intimately.

Key #19: Drop the Critical Self-Talk

No, Indigo, you are not going bananas. You actually do hear, see, feel, and sense things others don't experience. You are an expansive and aware intuitive being. Because we are very aware of our intuitiveness, we are equally aware that much of the world around us does not reflect or support that knowledge. That can trigger pain, frustration, anger, or anxiety inside our bodies and send our spirits plummeting. If we accept the lack of support that we see or hear around us, we shift into doubt mode and engage in negative self-talk. It is this self-talk that perpetuates the inner anxiety and effectively blocks the connection to spirit.

Telling yourself things that are opposite to how spirit speaks to you is a disservice to yourself. It is not the language of your spirit but of the ego instead. The ego is the critical voice of the mind that comes out just when you are on the verge of connecting with your essence. The closer you are to doing that and being true to your self, the louder and larger that ego voice becomes.

The voices of intuition and ego are distinct. Intuition is calm, quiet, and often subtle. Ego is loud, random, and anxious. It chatters continually and jumps around from topic to topic. Intuition is positive, loving, and feels solid. Ego is negative and operates from fear. It will always find reasons for you not to do something.

So start replacing those negative critical phrases with positive ones:

Negative	Positive
I doubt that…	I know.
I wonder if that's correct.	I know.

Negative	Positive
I'm not sure what I'm seeing. (feeling, hearing)	I see, I hear, I feel, I sense.
I can't…	I am. I do.
Yeah, but…	I know.
I don't know.	I know.
That's not true.	It is.
That couldn't be.	It is.
I must be crazy.	I am okay and perfect.
I am broken.	I am whole and perfect.

Knowing yourself consciously, as I outlined in chapter 10, is the first step to becoming confident with who you are and not allowing your ego self-talk to take control.

Key #20: Clear Your Mind to Hear Your Spirit

Your mind is powerful. It is constantly full of thoughts—not just your own but everything that you intuit from the mass consciousness of people around you. I listened to a Public Broadcasting Service program one evening where a prominent mind-body guru said that we have at least sixty thousand thoughts running through our minds daily. That is an astounding number. And very likely, we are not even consciously aware of at least 98 percent of those thoughts. Imagine that—sixty thousand! That gives you an idea of how busy our minds really are and how easy it can be to sabotage your spirit voice.

As with your energy system, you have control over this. Clearing your mind and monitoring the chatter allows you to focus on and hear when your spirit speaks or other intuitive information comes through.

The easy way to distinguish the mental chatter from your spirit is to know that the mental voices are loud and feel like they run all over the place or spring back and forth like a yo-yo; the spirit is subtle, more subdued, quieter, softer, solid, and never wavers. The following mental clearing process is simple and does not require a lot of time. It allows you to sit down and ground your energy as well.

1. Pick a favorite spot to sit comfortably.

2. Bring your awareness to your body. If there are any tense spots, let them relax.

3. Uncross your legs, place your feet flat on the floor, keep your back straight, and let your arms rest gently in your lap.

4. Take a deep breath through your nose, keeping your mouth closed. Relax your jaw.

5. Place your attention on your breath; note how it moves in and out.

6. Feel yourself relaxing more and more on each breath out.

7. Now visualize your breath coming in through your nose as white light. Breathe in the white light.

8. Allow this light to start filling your body—your cells, organs, muscles, and bones, until you are infiltrated by this bundle of white light.

9. Exhale out the gray clutter of the mind through your mouth. the clutter may be thoughts that arise in the middle of this exercise, the busyness of the day's events, feelings of fear, anxiety, or worries, or even thoughts about what you want to eat for dinner.

10. Repeat: Inhale white light through the nose, exhale gray clutter through your mouth.

11. You can repeat this for as long as it feels comfortable.

12. Sit for a while in this energy of light, feeling the attractive silence that has replaced the busy clutter.

13. When you feel you have relaxed and cleared sufficiently, bring yourself back into the present space and time.

Mental clearing takes practice. It's like training a puppy. You keep placing the puppy on the newspaper where you want it to go; it wanders away; you put it back, over and over again. This is conditioning. The mind functions the same way. If a myriad of thoughts creep in, simply shift your focus back to your breath and the light. Eventually you will get the hang of it, and it will get easier. After much practice, it will become second nature to you.

If you like, you can take this mental clearing to the next level and start to meditate and purposefully tune in to spirit.

Key #21: Tune In to Your Spirit through Meditation

Meditation is the art of mental control. It is an effective way to get in touch with your intuition and be in control of the process itself. It has the power to awaken us to our spirit as well as help us cope with the stresses in daily life.

There are many forms of meditation. This includes the stereotypical image that involves sitting cross-legged, closing your eyes, smelling incense, and chanting mantras. Do you have to do this to meditate? Only if you feel comfortable doing it. Many activities can be meditative: dancing; moving your body; doing exercises such as yoga or tai chi; sitting by the ocean; walking through the forest; playing music; painting or drawing; praying; or writing. These are all effective meditation techniques.

There are two basic parts to meditation: focus and breathing. By placing your focus on something, which may or may not include the breath, you are shifting away from the busy mental chatterbox to your inner self, your spirit, which is very quiet. The next phase after clearing your mind is to shift your focus onto the inner you—the quiet, subtle you—your spirit. This first part of this exercise embodies the mental clearing exercise that you did earlier.

1. Pick a favorite spot to sit comfortably.

2. Bring your awareness to your body. If there are any tense spots, let them relax.

3. Uncross your legs, place your feet flat on the floor, keep your back straight, and let your arms rest gently in your lap.

4. Take a deep breath through your nose, keeping your mouth closed. Relax your jaw.

5.   Place your attention on your breath; note how it moves in and out.

6.   Feel yourself relaxing more and more on each breath out.

7.   Visualize a ball of light, the color of a red ruby, right in the middle of your heart.

8.   See this ball of light spread outward from your heart and into your head, chest, arms, fingers, pelvis, legs, feet, and toes.

9.   Feel this light go deeply into your brain and envelop you.

10. Focus on this light.

11. This core energy is your spirit, the carrier of all knowledge and information. Connect with it. See what it feels like.

12. Connect with the silence and stillness of this light and hold your focus on it.

13. You may find yourself seeing pictures, hearing sounds, or sensing. That is perfectly okay.

14. If you do, this is a validation that you are consciously connected to your spirit.

15. Think of your connection to your spirit like a super-high-speed Internet. You plug in and connect. It is a connection that is there 24/7. You can access it any time you desire.

16. Feel the joy that is emanating through this connection.

17. Allow yourself to receive this unlimited and unconditional love and know that you can connect to this feeling any time and any place.

Just like the mind-centering exercises, using meditation to tune in to your spirit gets easier with practice. This is a fundamental aspect of honoring your spirit. The more you consciously remain connected to your spirit, the easier it will be for you, Indigo, to deal with stress, be honest with yourself, act on your intuition, and heal what stands in the way of expressing your true purpose.

Key #22: Trust Your Inner Knowing

As I write this, spring is here. The flowers are starting to bloom; the trees and bushes are budding. Signs of life and new growth are evident. But, just a mere month ago, in the very same spots where flowers are now seen, there was nothing visible but bare dirt. Yet, I knew that when I looked at the ground where I had planted my bulbs last fall that there was definitely something happening.

How did I know? Well, my intuition said that there was movement underneath. However, there was an integral piece to using that intuition, and that was trust. I had to trust that when I planted my flower bulbs in November that even though I wouldn't see anything with my eyes for at least three months, the bulb would produce a lovely blooming flower at some point. Trust is a vital component to honoring your spirit connection. It is the intangible piece that all too often is forgotten as we get swept up in the critical ego voices around us—our own or those of others.

There are three offshoots to trusting your intuitive voice:

1. **Accept what you intuit.** Accept the impression that comes first and foremost into your consciousness. What you are receiving is accurate unto itself. This involves removing the rational, logical, analyzing part of you. Remember the mental exercises? They will help you become more confident in trusting what you receive. Do not second guess just because the rational part of your mind may not understand. What you receive is how it's meant to be.

2. **Believe in yourself.** You are a powerful intuitive. It is your natural state of being. You, Indigo, bring that into this life as a gift to many people. You are here to anchor light onto this planet, by fully and consciously living in your purpose. This requires you to believe in your ability and to know who you are. Sometimes this can be a challenge, especially when hundreds if not thousands of other beliefs or behaviors swirl around you. That is exactly the challenge—believing in spite of all the

contradictions, unpopular and unsupported viewpoints, criticisms, rejections, and misunderstandings.

3.   **Act on what you intuit.** This is by the far the biggest piece of trust. Acting on what you intuitively receive requires a leap of faith. Just like trusting a flower bulb to produce a flower in its own time and in its own way, take the leap and put your hands into your spirit, rather than the confusing and critical ego voice.

I was well into my teenage years before I consciously realized that this ability of mine wasn't going away anytime soon. I just didn't know what to do with it or how to handle it. And I found it hard to act on my intuition as I got older, because I had no support structure. I had to learn to simply have faith and act on things without knowing the end result.

So, the more you practice clearing, connecting, and trusting, the easier it will be for you to survive in this world and to move forward in life with courage. Trusting and acting are the most courageous pieces of all of this.

Understanding the Indigo Mind-Body Connection

CHAPTER FIFTEEN

Seek the wisdom of the ages,
but look at the world through the eyes of a child.[18]

—Ron Wild
Author

There are two important aspects relating to the physical and mental well-being of an Indigo:

1. Because the energy system of an Indigo is highly expanded (as set out in chapter 13 in the thirteen-chakra system), an Indigo's vibration is also highly accelerated. Because the body and mind are also energy, they too vibrate much more quickly. This "quickness" shows up physically and mentally in several ways—being mentally speedy, understanding concepts at lightning speed, speaking quickly with disjointed sentences (starting one sentence before finishing another), consistently multitasking and accomplishing much in a short period of time, and physically needing to move around while talking, thinking, or focusing on something else.

2.   Healing the spiritual, mental, emotional, and physical levels are vital. The most external of the four is the physical body. Because Indigos are very much in tune with the energies of others and feel everything (they are not disassociated from their feelings), they equally feel every nuance of discord in their bodies.

Key #23: Bodily Movement is the Key to Mental Focus

The latter characteristic is especially important, because it speaks to the heart of many misdiagnoses of attention deficit disorder and attention deficit hyperactivity disorder. While it is important to understand that not every diagnosis is incorrect, the energy system of most Indigo children is constantly in motion and not meant to be held motionless. Being forced to cease being in motion equates to boredom for an Indigo, and that is like the kiss of death. That is why many have difficulty sitting still to focus—because they are energetically meant not to sit still. Indigos can bring themselves to focus at will—simply by choosing to.

It has been scientifically shown that when performing a boring task, the prefrontal cortex of the brain changes, and the brain essentially shuts down. In addition, boredom to an Indigo often is triggered from a lack of free choice leading to a lack of fun, and then to boredom. If this were stated like a visual equation, that connection would look like this:

Lack of freedom to choose → Uninteresting activity → Motionless → Boredom → Brain shutdown

Indigos need to work in the opposite direction. They *need* bodily movement or physical stimulation to focus and achieve mental stimulation and interest—not the other way around. In other words, they are not deficient in attention but actually have a surplus. It is that surplus that is evident in their outward need to physically move, all the time, especially when performing a task or trying to listen to or focus on something.

To help the Indigo make his or her way in this world, finding supportive systems that involve physical healing and movement are essential. Educational and home environments need to place their energy on promoting systems that are more conducive to the Indigo's energy system, as well as understanding their unique characteristics and needs.

To date, this has been challenging to caregivers, teachers, and parents, because current systems advocate children sitting still to focus on something in particular—eating, learning, listening, talking. Even bedtime can be a hurdle, especially when a child is still running at full speed.

Here's a hard truth: It is perfectly natural to fidget and move around. Movement is essential for brain stimulation. We as biological beings cannot sit still for any significant length of time. Because an Indigo's energy system is constantly vibrating at a higher speed, that translates to an even greater need for physical movement and less sitting still. More often than not, young Indigos can be the bane of the school classroom, *not* sitting still and paying attention, but instead running around, seemingly being disruptive and all over the place. These are some of the many reasons why Indigos feel misunderstood by those in authority, especially in an educational system where physical movement and focus do not typically go together.

The key here is to find effective ways to physically move and therefore focus. These strategies include sound, sight, and unobtrusive rhythmic body movement through touch.

Visual strategies can include locking eyes on something specific around you, such as an object, animal, or person. Simply move your gaze briefly away from what you are trying to focus on, look at another the object, and then quickly move your focus back.

I discovered the importance of this strategy when trying to maintain eye contact with people for more than ten seconds at a time. I just couldn't do it. The problem is that maintaining eye contact when speaking with someone is important and usually engenders a sense of honesty and integrity. Shifting your gaze away from the person that your attention is on sends the opposite message. As Indigos, we often need to briefly shift our gaze. It is necessary to continuously snap back into a focused place. When Indigos do this, they are not being rude, dishonest, or inattentive. It is just their accelerated energy at work and a visual need to keep their brains stimulated and in focus.

Auditory strategies are especially common with Indigos. They need background music, nature sounds, or "white noise," such as passing traffic. Sometimes they need to talk to themselves. These strategies are vital for bringing the Indigo brain to a focused place.

It took me well into my college years before I recognized that it was my classical pianist training that gave me my great ability to maintain focus, my long-term memory retention, and my ability to quickly retrieve mental information from as far back as early childhood and infancy.

While studying for exams, I always needed music to drive information into my memory. At test time, I would retrieve that same information through mental music triggers. I would recall the music—words or tune—and that would trigger my memory bank and hasten my information recall.

While writing this book, I worked in a room with several computers. At any given time, there was either gentle music playing in the background to help me whenever I had a mental block or the hum of the second computer. This was enough of a trigger to keep me mentally on target.

Kinesthetic or tactile strategies are usually pertinent for more sedate or quiet activities such as reading or working at a desk. Because jumping up and running around a classroom may not necessarily be appropriate, the tactile or touch aspect becomes important.

During my coaching sessions with individuals, I need to hold onto something with my hands while speaking. I take notes during client sessions, and if I'm not writing, I have to at least hold my pen. The touch of the pen in my hand, or the act of reaching for a cup of tea, or drinking tea can serve as a focal anchor. I would feel entirely naked, bored, and distracted without them.

This explains why many children doodle in class, move their hands, chew gum, and look like they are not paying attention. They simply need tactile/kinesthetic activity to keep themselves stimulated and focused.

Key #24: It Is Essential to Heal on All Levels

We are blessed to be spiritual beings in physical bodies. We are also blessed to have a mind that thinks. Although energy management is a large aspect of helping Indigos survive, the reality is that we are here in a body—a human body. We have chosen on a soul level to take on the physical cloak to experience life in a new and different way—to feel emotions, to learn lessons, to ultimately accelerate our growth, and to expand our awareness as a soul being.

One of the big challenges for Indigos is being able to exist in their physical bodies. The experience is often painful—a pain that originates not on the bodily level but on the spiritual level. The state of our inner knowledge does not match the state of the external world. Pain resulting from the recognition of the disparity between the two sits in the energy of the Indigo. The struggle, therefore, is trying to handle functioning with a human body in a chaotic world, while at the same time being tapped into the inner knowledge of a higher, loving, perfect vision of the world.

Much of this painful memory gets downloaded from the eighth chakra—the chakra in the Indigo-Crystal system that carries past-life information and karmic residue or miasms. Although the word typically is used in the context of illness and disease, miasms are usually considered to be heredity patterns that are passed along from previous lifetimes into the current one. In this case, miasms are karmic imprints that we become aware of more consciously.

Many of the older Indigos who are coming into their third, fourth, or fifth decade of life and are waking up consciously to what they are meant to be doing have gone through the process of cleaning up and healing past-life residue that has been brought forward into this life. Young Indigos and even Crystals within their first five years of life often experience night terrors or nightmares, primarily because they cannot discern the difference between past-life and current life experiences, especially at night when their spirit temporarily disassociates from their little bodies.

Sometimes the pain is great and the emotions overwhelming. Depression, aggression, grief, rage, anxiety, hopelessness, and fear are not uncommon, especially among Indigo teens who are trying to discover their identity and place in the world. Unresolved emotional and spiritual pain usually manifest into physical pain.

Through many years as a holistic health practitioner, I have worked with clients who have had complex disorders such as fibromyalgia or lupus. I found a myriad of symptoms with no apparent cause. I concluded that unresolved spiritual or emotional pain was the underlying cause.

I discovered two important things. The first was that every person with autoimmune challenges showed trauma patterns to some degree. During treatment, I typically connect with a person's soul, and almost every one of those clients displayed painful memories and thought beliefs from either their current life or previous lifetimes.

The second awareness came from working with adult Indigos. In my client base, nine out of ten clients reveal a history of either not being hugged or lacking positive physical contact from a young age.

During the intense healing period from my own health issues, I uncovered buried memories and angry feelings at not being touched for at least the first month after my premature birth. I was an incubator baby, and as flash after flash of pictures ran through my mind like a movie, I was shown how it was possible for an intense emotion like anger to exist even at such a young age and to remain in the body for decades. The fibromyalgia pain and chronic fatigue that I carried around for years, much of which I held in my muscle, bones, and joints, was connected with my anger at the absence of touch in the early months and years of my life. Later on, when I was physically abused, I absorbed the negativity passed on by my mother's abusive acts. My body absorbed the energy, and it eventually grew into pain. In the end, to get on with what I came here to do, I chose not to fall victim to my circumstances. After all, as a soul, I had a hand in choosing the situation that I grew up with.

Looking back, the pain and physical disorders were what helped shape and strengthen me. I had to take responsibility for my health, my energy, and my physical body. This life was the only one that I had. It was up to me to take care of it and heal anything and everything that prevented me from fully expressing my purpose.

I have noticed that many Indigos do not come into fully functional families. Their souls will often choose families that have some form of major chaos or upheaval, such as separation and divorce or substance addiction. This choice is not intended to overwhelm the Indigo, but instead to allow for experience of these chaotic scenarios to strengthen the spirit, turn the challenges into constructive purpose, and encourage rapid growth as individuals, so they can become the leaders that Indigos naturally are.

How do we address this need? We are living in the twenty-first century, and the concept of mind-body connection has come into the forefront as an acceptable viewpoint of how to approach physical and mental health and healing. More modalities are available than ever before, and new forms are constantly being created. What has been shown to me over and over again is the need to integrate healing through all levels of being. Focusing on one level just isn't good enough. All levels—physical, mental, emotional, and spiritual—have to be honored.

Although there are hundreds of therapies and alternative modalities available, a few stand out, and I offer here an overview of seven—as suggestions only, not recommendations. Only you will know what you gravitate toward and desire to implement in your life. Use your intuition to guide you.

Yoga

This is one of the oldest known health practices in the world. The principle behind yoga is this: If the mind is anxious, then physical health will be at risk; if the body is compromised, mental health will be adversely affected. The idea behind practicing yoga is to bring all parts of the body, mind, and spirit into balance through poses, stretches, meditations, and breath work.

YogaKids is a company that creates creative exercise DVDs and videos just for children, geared perfectly for Indigo and Crystal children, and adults too. This is a great way for parents to support their Indigos in using their body and integrating mind and spirit.

Neuromuscular Integrative Action (NIA)

Combining the concepts of yoga, martial arts, and nine dance movements, this practice uses the body to heal the mind, emotions, and spirit by joining conscious muscular movement with introspection, visualization, imagery, and expression. This helps a person become conscious of their body and the emotions stored within. Verbal language is often used to express what comes forward during the practice of NIA, thereby bringing into awareness feelings that have been buried in the body.

Regularly practicing NIA may help relieve depression, post-traumatic stress disorder, anxiety, substance addictions, and abusive behaviors.

Tai Chi and Qigong

Both Tai Chi and qigong are ancient Chinese exercises that connect with qi, the life-force energy that makes up who we are. They help stimulate and balance the flow through energy pathways or meridians of the body. Both help harmonize the mind and spirit and assist the body in returning to its natural state of balance.

Both exercises, although slightly different in execution, are similar in that they combine multibody movements with meditation, visualization, and breath coordination to promote relaxation, thereby affecting the whole body positively. Both exercises cost little to learn or to do.

Neuro-Linguistic Programming (NLP)

Although not specifically a physical exercise, NLP, also known as neurolinguistic psychology, can have an effect on the physical body. By focusing on how people communicate, think, learn, and grow, NLP can help reprogram unconscious patterns of language, thought, and beliefs about oneself to heal and alter psychological response.

Indigos carry karmic residue into this life, and part of the Dark Night of the Soul process is to clear and heal everything that was carried forward into the present. To tap into and fully express one's authenticity, anything that stands in the way—fears, false beliefs, identifications, life goals that don't fit with deep desires, physical sensitivities, and health issues—can be identified and redirected with NLP.

Underlying traumas that come in through past-life memory or present-life events are imprinted in the body from an early age. Remember my example earlier about not being touched in the first month of life? That was an emotional trauma that was imprinted on my body and stayed there for several decades until I took responsibility and decided that it no longer needed to reside there. After that, through NLP and other treatment modalities, my fibromyalgia pain, anxiety, depression, and chronic fatigue were drastically reduced and now are barely perceptible.

NLP practitioners can be found around the globe. If your intention is to work and heal the core, then finding a practitioner who is trained in the physical aspect of healing is vital.

Emotional Freedom Technique (EFT)

A relatively new form of energetic treatment, EFT is innovative, yet based on old concepts of acupuncture—with a twist. Energy points on the body—the ones on which acupuncture is based—are tapped with the fingertips instead of needles. The idea is to release the negative pattern of thinking that is lodged in that area of the body and replace it with a positive thought or belief.

Thousands of people have found relief from many types of diseases, pain, and emotional issues through the practice of EFT. It is an extremely effective technique to practice, anytime and anywhere, and is cost-effective. For more information, see the resources section of this book.

Reiki and Healing Touch

Reiki, a Japanese healing technique that promotes stress reduction, wellness, and relaxation, is a laying on of hands on the body, through which universal life-force energy is guided. Reiki typically treats the whole person—-mind, emotions, body, and spirit.

Similar to Reiki, Healing Touch is considered a form of biofield therapy and influences the human energy system by touching the body. Founded by a registered nurse, Healing Touch is practiced by a range of people and is widely accepted in the mainstream medical arena.

Music and Mozart

There has been a new buzz word floating around since the 1990s—-The Mozart Effect. The concept is old but recently rediscovered and controversial. How can a young Austrian composer have an effect on our society 250 years after his birth? Simple. It has been proven that music and memory relate, and that music has a great impact on memory. Mozart, with his happy, simple melodies and uplifting tunes, has been revived in the late twentieth and early twenty-first centuries.

Music plays a vital role in a child's learning process. I can say with confidence that if it were not for my classical musical training background, I would have had a much more difficult time developing my psychic abilities, especially in the visual and auditory fields. Classical music allowed me to develop my spatial and reasoning abilities quickly and assisted me in focusing, concentrating, and dealing with stress and anxiety and moving toward better mental health.

Memory has been shown to significantly improve when the brain is subjected to specific types of music—classical music and especially composers like Mozart. Research within the last fifteen years suggests that listening to music repeatedly increases a child's spatial intelligence (reasoning, puzzle solving, mental imaging, visual acuity) and even school test scoring. *Prevention Magazine* reported in February 1994 that, "Research found that inner-city children's reasoning skills that tested below the U.S. average doubled after listening to music."

Classical music has again become popular, bringing the old into the new. Companies such as Baby Einstein have exposed the importance of classical music and its effects on children's intelligence, mental development, and spiritual well-being through many visual and audio products. More information can be found in the resources section of this book.

There is no one route to healing or determining what is right for you. Simply know that everything in life has a connection—body, emotions, mind, and spirit. Any healing facilitated on one level will have an effect on all of them. The key is simple: Just start and the rest will follow. Your whole being will thank you for it.

Key #25: Don't Take Yourself Too Seriously

As an Indigo, you can have a very serious side; can feel the intense gamut of emotions; an may want to fight against things you believe to be wrong, broken, dysfunctional, or in need change. You can connect with someone's soul and intuit information through direct eye contact. Yet, you also know that life overall was not meant to be serious. You are a part of life. Therefore you contribute directly to how life looks and evolves, including your own.

So laugh at yourself. Have fun. Life is short, and you have a purpose to fulfill. And yes, your purpose is important. But you can choose to fulfill it with utter seriousness or with joy and light-heartedness.

If Snoopy, the beagle extraordinaire from the *Peanuts* comic strip, can fulfill his purpose by lying on top of his doghouse, then you can do likewise.

HELP, I HAVE AN INDIGO. WHAT DO I DO?

PART IV

Seven Tips for Indigo Guidance
CHAPTER SIXTEEN

Each child is an adventure into a better life—an opportunity to
change the old pattern and make it new.[19]

—Hubert Humphrey
Thirty-eighth vice president of the United States

As I write this book, our school system seems to be collapsing before our very eyes. More and more frustrated educators are trying to deal with seemingly difficult behaviors in and out of the classroom. More and more parents are pulling their children out of mainstream public schools and placing them in alternative schools such as Montessori and Waldorf. Some are homeschooling. Behavioral challenges are on the rise at home, in schools, and in society at large.

What is happening? Is it the children? Is it the school? Is it the home environment? Is it society that is contributing to the so-called chaos? The answer lies in the fundamental beliefs that underlie all of the above.

If you are reading this book, chances are that you are a parent of an Indigo child or know of someone who is. Or perhaps you have identified children in your care or classroom as potential Indigos, whether they are primary school age, preteen, or teen. As a parent, teacher, or caregiver, you probably have experienced frustration at the many strategies that have not worked with your Indigo. Whether through communication or just general interaction, you are wondering how to handle or understand your Indigo. Because let's face it, for the first two decades of an Indigo's life, parents are the prime guiding force in their lives. Educators and caregivers also have a hand in supporting how these children evolve.

This section offers tips and strategies on how to better understand, communicate with, and interact with Indigo children, whether they are in your home, classroom, day care, or any other environment.

Infant and Young Indigos

Let's start small. We are all born with tiny bodies but great love. What parent hasn't experienced profound joy and awe when a baby was born? From that point onward, you begin the journey of discovering your child. You have the opportunity to embark on a new paradigm of parenting.

From the moment an Indigo is born, he or she comes into this world immersed in divine love. *Isn't that true for all of us?* Yes, it is!

Almost all parents of Indigos that I have spoken with have shared with me that when their Indigo children were born, there was a sense of profound awe, wonder, and peace that prevailed upon them. I can include myself when I say that when my daughter was born, I strongly felt that I was in the presence of a great and wise being. I was deeply humbled.

Some Indigos arrive encased in peace. And some arrive ready to be the strong warrior that they are. Either way, they come in on this earthly journey knowing that they are here with full cooperation between themselves and God. The challenges lie in young Indigos learning to be themselves in the face of a world that does not match how they know their true selves to be. As a parent, caregiver, or educator living in a world that is bound by rules, systems, and paradigms, this requires a lot of patience, openness, and willingness to set aside your own judgments and preconceived notions.

Preteen, Teen, and Adolescent Indigos

The teenage Indigo, like any other child entering their second decade of life, starts facing and trying to answer the ultimate question: *Who am I?* This is the prime time for starting to adjust to life—finding their identity; developing socially and emotionally; recognizing how they fit and where they belong in the world; learning how to respond to rules and structures around them; and determining what they believe or value, just for starters.

The only difference between Indigo teens and others is that they come into this life aware of the disparity between the world they see around them and what they carry inside. In this stage of life development, they are even more conscious of that disparity.

Armed with greater verbal and cognitive development, Indigo teens are aware that they have much more control and capacity to start doing something about making change and protesting against issues, behaviors, words, beliefs, or actions that are not showing integrity or do not align with respect, peace, harmony, equality, collaboration, and cooperation.

It is often during this time that Indigos experience mood swings, become more sensitive to emotions, foods, chemicals, or non-natural substances. It is important as parents, caregivers, and educators to understand what is happening to Indigos during this time and to support them through these experiences with tolerance and without judgment.

Tip #1: Show them honor and respect.

Aretha Franklin said it best—*respect yourself.* This statement can be applied to anyone, young or old. Unfortunately, our pervasive societal belief system has not allowed for respecting children. The paradigm that most of us have been taught is to honor and respect your elders, teachers, and parents. Children are to be seen and not heard. Only those who were older—well past childhood—and had accumulated a vast amount of earthly experience were the only ones deemed worthy of respect. Wisdom and children were never put together.

Indigo children, and even non-Indigos children, are very wise. Yes, they are young, but they came into life with a vast accumulation of soul knowledge and awareness. Many Indigos carry lifetimes of experience.

Treating them as equals from that level is necessary for their well-being and their process through life. If you don't show that respect toward them and instead talk down to them, they will know it, resent it, and will not reciprocate with respect.

Indigos will unequivocally suffer if their worthiness is not acknowledged. Some shift into violent, criminal actions; have thoughts or acts of suicide; depend on drugs or other substances to numb their inner pain; and disassociate emotionally, mentally, and spiritually. Their pain is directly linked with the lack of respect and fairness shown to them.

Indigos come into this life from the confident place of understanding that all beings are created equal. But it is important as a guide to acknowledge them in return with fairness and equality. They are awesome beings with great things to offer this world. Acknowledge that. They do not ask for anything less.

Tip #2: Structure is important but so is freedom to choose.

Allow equal contribution in both your household and your teaching environment. Indigos will instantly, and I mean instantly, detect when their freedom to choose *anything* is violated. Young Indigos may not consciously know that this issue lies at the core of their distress and often will have difficulty communicating it.

Giving them the freedom to choose does *not* equate to the absence of structure, limits, or boundaries. Children need and want structure when they are growing up. It teaches them about frameworks, boundaries, and ways of learning to relate to the world around them.

For example, my daughter's school has a hot lunch program. A two-week menu is given out several weeks ahead of time with descriptions of ten meals. Katerina, who is aware of her sensitivities to specific foods, chooses which meals she would like to have at school. The structure and limits are there, and she has freedom of choice within that structure. She is content, because she is included in the decision-making process, and I am happy as a parent because there is a structure in place from which to operate from.

Another area where choice and structure can work together is trying to get your child to sleep. Indigos and Crystal children often resist sleep, because of their active, high-energy patterns. Their energy will just not settle down! If you are a parent, this can be frustrating, especially if you have preconceived ideas of when a child should go to sleep or for how long. There may be a clash between your time-bound notions and the child's natural inner clock.

With Indigos and Crystals, neither domination nor guilt will work. Don't try to tell your child, "You should go to bed now, because I say so," (domination) or, "You better go to bed, or you'll be tired in the morning and have dark circles under your eyes" (guilt. The quick response is usually an emphatic no. Their behavior will be anything but related to getting ready for bed. Indigos will usually buck this system, knowing internally that they are not governed by the human constructs of clock or calendar time. Instead, they are on their own time and will make sure that they stick to it no matter what.

So, how do you as a parent or caregiver show responsibility, yet respect the Indigo's natural energy patterns? By dropping the "shoulds, coulds, and woulds." Instead, cocreate a structure that incorporates their participation.

First, they need to know that they are here on earth, which is governed by human clock time. Second, a balance between the clock rhythm and the child's inner rhythm needs to be established.

Differentiating between bedtime and sleep time is one way of approaching it, especially for younger Indigos. Again, I will use my daughter, Katerina, as an example. She contributed to creating her effective structure. She begins getting ready for bed at about 8:30 PM. She begins winding down. The actual bedtime is closer to 9:00 PM. At that time, she may brush her hair, put on her pajamas, read a story, listen to quiet nature music, or have a massage. The sleep time occurs around 10:00 or 10:30, when lights go out.

As a parent, I want my child to get enough sleep. That is normal and natural. We all want the best for our children. At the same time, knowing she is a Crystal child whose energy just cannot settle down according to the rules of human clock time, I need to respect her natural rhythms and her desire to relax at her own pace. By including her in the decision, we cocreated a structure that works for her, and everyone is happier all around.

For younger Indigos, give them structure but allow them choice and respect their equal contribution. To Indigo children, this is a black-and-white issue. Acknowledging their freedom to choose *is* respecting and hearing them.

As for teenager and adolescent Indigos, at a time where identities and roles in life are being explored and carved out, the balance between freedom to choose and structure is equally vital. It is important to listen to what your child is communicating to you—with an open mind and heart.

And there is already slight progress in the educational system to reflect this. Cable News Network (CNN) reported that as of March 23, 2006, legislation was passed in the State of Florida that allows high school students may pick major and minor courses of studies which allows them to design their lives of their own volition. By listening to what students had to say about their future, their dreams and visions for their lives, school systems have taken steps to acknowledge that, yet still keeping to specific structure.

My desire that children are honored and respected for their visions, become reality everywhere.

Tip #3: Communicate clearly and behave honestly, fairly, and with integrity.

Maintain eye contact and be direct in your communication without any guilt trips or manipulation tactics. Indigos can sniff out deceitful behavior or superficiality. Indigos have lie detectors built right into their systems. You can't put anything over on them, so don't even try.

Indigos are intelligent and show great maturity compared to others their age. Try to give complete and honest explanations for everything. Even the most complicated issue can be explained simply for young children. The bottom line is they want reasons from you. It displays authenticity and honesty.

Indigos do not accept the notion of blindly doing things. "Because I said so," or, "Just do it," won't work. They always need to know and understand why they are being asked to do something, and they need to understand the underlying purpose. Otherwise the request is meaningless to them. So always explain. Even a simple form will do.

Tip #4: Acknowledge and support their intuitive abilities and higher knowledge.

Being intuitive and sensitive is normal for an Indigo. Just as we all are, They are psychic beings, but they arrive with their psychic abilities open and intact. It isn't until they start to get older that Indigos become aware that other people around them do not necessarily share their experiences or show their abilities. Indigos are tapped in to many levels of awareness. It is part of who they are, and they consciously know it and show it. Do not discount or negate what comes out of their mouths. It is not in their imagination. Acknowledge and accept the "normalcy," despite the fact that it may run contrary to what you believe or feel.

Respect the fact that they talk to angels, spirits, dead people, and God. They can, as we all can and do! Suspending your judgments around this is important in supporting them.

Another way to support them is to help develop their abilities by exposing them to intuitive training and classes. Because Indigos are plugged in to other people's emotions, it is vital that they learn grounding, shielding, relaxation, and healing techniques. Some techniques can be found in chapter 13 on Energy Management.

Be aware that especially during the teenage Indigo years, mood swings often occur because of improper or absent shielding and grounding of their own energy.

As a result they absorb too much energy of others, and it causes their energy system to become imbalanced, thus translating to intense and wild mood shifts.

Tip #5: Be aware of and tolerant of their physical sensitivities.

The energy system of an Indigo is usually sensitive. That often translates to being physically sensitive as well. There are two aspects to this:

- It is important to listen to your child, especially when it comes to food and what goes into their bodies.
- Their systems are sensitive and "dead" food, such as processed, refined, packaged, or canned foods, have a negative effect on them.

Children are very honest communicators. Indigos are no exception, but they tend to be blunt. They will tell you when a particular food doesn't work with them—whether they don't like something or just won't eat it. That does not mean that they have complete and utter freedom in their food choices. It is *still* important to communicate to them why chocolate and candy are not one of the major food groups. Structure with choice plays a strong part in this as well.

Avoid the dominator push-pull approach. "Eat your beans, because they are good for you" is an old model and usually does not work with them. Instead, ask your child what he or she feels is bothering them about the particular food. Including them in the process is vital.

Their physical sensitivities also include non-food things, such as being exposed to loud or grating noises, synthetic materials, non-natural fabrics, tags, chemicals, pesticides, metals, and electrical objects, such as watches or clocks. Many of these are grating or irritating to an Indigo's energy system. When they fuss about tags rubbing against their skin or complain about wearing something that just "doesn't feel right," they are not kidding. They experience it as jarring and non-harmonious to their systems. Listen to them. They know best what they are experiencing.

Tip #6: Recognize that Indigos' opinions are worthy.

This goes right up there with respect. Respecting an Indigo's opinions communicates the message that you see them as worthy, as well as shows that you care about what they think.

There is no Indigo excluded from this. Big or small, their knowledge is valuable. Listen to them with an open heart and mind. Do not interrupt them. Suspend your judgment when they are talking back, being argumentative, or becoming difficult.

Like all children, young Indigos will be developing their communication skills and do not always express themselves politely. However, they will be honest and direct. They are direct, because they know who they are internally and have no need to hide or mask their feelings. Their honesty reveals different angles and viewpoints to situations.

So be patient, open, and receptive to what they have to say. They, too, are persons of great value. You just might end up seeing and learning something new.

Tip #7: Help them to cultivate their purpose for being here.

Throughout this book, I have written about purpose—why Indigos are here. Indigos are peacemakers. As the Bible says in Matthew 5:9 (NRSV), "Blessed are the peacemakers; for they shall be called the children of God."[20] Indigos truly embody this phrase.

Anchoring light on this planet and helping make the world a better place is an enormous task and responsibility. Indigos are up to the challenge or they wouldn't be here at such a crucial time. Making a difference is the Indigo motto. As an Indigo supporter in whatever capacity that may be—parent, caregiver, teacher, family member, or friend—it is important to understand that making a difference is their mission. How they express that purpose will develop and be discovered over time.

You can help them discover and cultivate their vision and purpose by encouraging their creativity and unique expression. They are not children who come from the linear view that they are here to grow up, go to school, acquire good grades, get in an even better school, and ultimately get a great-paying job and be financially successful. Their purpose is larger than making money or competing to achieve top school grades. They are children who get frustrated when they see issues like poverty, mental illness, abuse, or homelessness.

Acknowledge their frustration. Help them find their voice and communicate their feelings with compassion. Several years ago, Katerina suddenly became passionate about contributing to the anti-poverty effort in Africa after seeing a television program about it. Her sadness about children being hungry and homeless resonated strongly with her. Now at age nine she helps contribute by saving some of her allowance and working with her school to send supplies and educational resources wherever they are needed.

Being a peacemaker is about being active, not passive. As Indigo guides and supporters, it is vital that you maintain an active role in cultivating their purpose. And if you can do that, you will have helped them survive—with flying colors.

QUESTIONS AND ANSWERS
PART V

Readers' Questions Answered
CHAPTER SEVENTEEN

You know children are growing up when they start asking questions
that have answers.[21]

—John J. Plomp
Author

Ever since I fully stepped into my Indigo-Crystal self, I have had the great pleasure of connecting with some amazing souls. Many are still searching to find their ways, to discover their purposes. Many are also waking up to the joy that they are not alone anymore and are finally understood.

I've received wonderful e-mails from so many people around the globe having a multitude of comments and questions. Thank you for all of them. Reading e-mail after e-mail, it was abundantly clear to me that a pattern was emerging. Many readers and writers shared similar stories and questions that need addressing.

Most of these topics have been addressed to some degree in this book, but I would like to share some answers to specific questions. Changes have been made to protect the writers' identities and to condense the content.

From a young adult Indigo:

Q: I am an artist, and I think I'm an Indigo. I have a natural talent for drawing, painting, and other expressions. This isn't enough for me to feel fulfilled in my life. I feel as if I'm meant to do other things—some bigger. I like the thought of being a counselor, but I do not enjoy going to a conventional educational institution like college. I'm bored sitting in classes. I feel frustrated, because the only way it seems that I can achieve anything is to attend a structured educational system. This is very restrictive for me. I am intuitive and would like to work with people, especially children. How do I figure out which way to go, and what I am meant to be doing in my life?

A: First, I commend you on discovering your true self. Part of the Indigo process is waking up to who you really are and honoring it. Talents typically show themselves early in life, giving clues to what your purpose is. Being Indigo, however, usually involves two levels of purpose. The first is a personal one. Usually this involves going through challenges or hurdles in life to learn lessons, helping to discover yourself and clearing out any blocks that prevent you from being fully in your next level. That level is one of a global nature. Often, Indigos need to go through the personal process before they are ready to take the next step and fulfill their global mission.

There is no right or wrong choice. Everything is choice. Your heart will always guide you in the direction that is aligned with your spirit. Your spirit holds the knowing of what your missions are in this life. The way you feel toward something is a clue about how in or out of alignment you are with your purpose. Sometimes we engage in struggle, because the external world holds opinions or judgment about what is considered appropriate and acceptable. Look into your heart. What is your heart telling you? Ask yourself if doing something brings you joy and a smile to your face, or does it feel like a drain? You will always have many talents and skills that bring you joy. However your multilevel purpose will always be connected with both your own personal growth and the lives of others.

From a parent of a young Indigo child:

Q: I believe my child may be an Indigo, and she has been diagnosed with ADHD. I do not want to give her synthetic medication like Ritalin. I've done some research on alternate remedies and treatments. Could something like homeopathy or the Bach Flower Remedies help?

A: It's wonderful that you have been blessed with an Indigo child in your life. Even though all children are "special" and come in with a purpose, Indigos certainly can pose a challenge, especially in the behavioral department.

Doreen Virtue, who wrote *The Care and Feeding of Indigo Children*, says that ADHD stands for Attention Dialed into a Higher Dimension. Indigo children are attuned to many dimensions. Imagine turning on your radio and receiving many stations simultaneously. Within a short time, a matter of seconds mostly likely, this could drive a person bonkers. Another way of understanding this is through what I call the "hourglass" analogy. Picture an hourglass—many streams of information are coming into the wide, top part of the hourglass and then are trying to funnel through the narrow channel in the middle. That is what happens to the Indigo brain and body. Large amounts of energy try to squeeze into a much narrower channel, creating an overload. For Indigos, this is a normal, daily occurrence. Figuring out how to handle this can be challenging for all—the parent, the caregiver, and of course, the child.

Bach Flower Remedies work on the premise that your ills are directly related to your negative state of mind, and cures can be achieved by replacing the negative state of mind with its opposite, balance and harmony. Flower remedies correspond to specific moods, states of mind, and personality traits. They have a direct effect on the personality, specifically on the emotional and mental levels. Homeopathy works in a similar way on the premise that "like cures like."

Because of the intense brain hyperactivity in Indigo children, "calm" is the operative word. At best, administering Bach Flower Remedies, such as the all-purpose Rescue Remedy, can have a stabilizing and calming effect, especially in stress-induced and traumatic situations. It also can help in situations like visiting the dentist or conquering stage-fright. The same applies to homeopathic preparations such as Chamomilla (chamomile flower). Any remedy should be assessed on an individual basis.

For Indigos, however, it is important to recognize that unlike illness or ailments, this is not a condition that will disappear. This is the natural state of their being. I strongly advocate a clean, healthy diet. For example, sugar, processed and refined foods, additives, preservatives, artificial colors, and caffeine all have a strong, often negative effect on all levels of being, especially for these children. This needs to be monitored carefully at all times, especially in the early formative years.

From parents of an Indigo teenager:

Q: I have a strong Indigo teen at home. She started piano lessons when she was a grade-schooler and fought me most of the way. When we moved, we sold the piano. Years later, she is suddenly interested in music. She saved her money for a used keyboard and is suddenly playing classical music that is far too complicated for her—but it is beautiful! She wants to take piano lessons again, but they are financially out of the question. That frustrated her for only a short time before she started teaching herself even more complicated musical pieces. She has even started guitar and recorder on her own, and she is progressing at an amazing rate. It's almost spooky! My question is: Is it her being an Indigo that makes this musical "magic" happen, or is it more like those past-life things I've read about where memories (like musical skills) are remembered?

A: First I want to commend you for obviously having the wonderful and courageous role of taking care of an Indigo child, especially one who is a teenager. Kudos to you! Second, I want to address your questions from the direction of past-life memory and what we all bring in to subsequent lives, whether we are Indigos or not.

First of all, we as soul beings carry all of our memory, learning, and experiences throughout every life we choose to go through. And I stress the word "choose," for we as soul beings also carry free will throughout every life, whether it's on Earth or beyond. This includes choosing consciously to go through the human experience, along with choosing the lessons, experiences, skills, talents, and themes that we will carry in that life. Sylvia Browne has written much along these lines in terms of what we as souls do on the other side before coming here in body form. I recommend her book, *Life on the Other Side*.

Your child, in addition to being an Indigo, has chosen creativity and creative expression as part of her life theme in this life. Part of that includes the memory of being a gifted musician, as well as a teacher of music in previous lives. So the short answer to your past-life inquiry is that your daughter is simply remembering what she has already mastered in previous times, hence the rapid progress.

The reason why she is suddenly waking up now is that she is at a time in her Indigo process where she is becoming more conscious of who she is and of her purposes in life. She is doing this consciously, in her own way, in her own time, when she is more fully able to embrace the knowing that she chose this as part of her path. This is not to say that in this life she will be a professional musician. However, I definitely see music as one mode of self-expression for her. And being the strong, heady Indigo that she is, the need to stand out and express that Indigo-ness in a strong and obvious way is vital. Music is one creative channel for that self-expression.

I would also like to say that the teenage years are crucial for children, particularly because they are figuring out where they fit in life, as well discovering who they are within themselves. This is a time among Indigo children when it is common to see major bouts of depression, and sometimes extreme anger, rage, or violence. Sometimes these intense emotions lead to drug and alcohol usage. That may happen when teenagers lack outlets to express themselves in safe, positive, and healthy ways.

It is good that your daughter has a safe, positive, creative outlet to discover herself. Keep encouraging and supporting her! And remember, Mozart was an Indigo too. Who knows, your daughter just might surprise you and be a new and improved Wolfgang Amadeus Mozart.

From a parent of an Indigo teenager:

Q: My Indigo daughter is very intelligent, but her grades in school don't reflect this. As a matter of fact, the chances are good that she will fail the year and have to repeat. Why is she doing this? I am so frustrated! I have shown patience and understanding, but she refuses to buckle down and study. Instead, she complains about the incompetence of the faculty. She's right, but that's not how the game is played. She's already repeated once. How can I make her understand before it's too late?

A: I feel your frustration as a parent wanting what is best for your child. This is an all-too-common scenario among young Indigos. Your highly intelligence daughter who makes low grades may be bored. Indigos often are bored within typical educational structures, because they are in a system where they feel forced to learn information that may not resonate with them. They may feel that it has no purpose in their lives, or perhaps the material and course are not creative enough to stimulate and excite them.

Furthermore, in the mainstream system there is a great focus on core or mandatory courses that everybody must complete successfully. The instructors are trained to think, perceive, and believe in accordance with the system. A very bored Indigo trying to find herself and the deeper purpose to everything may perceive this as incompetent. Unfortunately, while the latter notion is not necessarily true, since Indigos can "sniff out" superficialities, they will respond to those superficialities the best way they know how—simply put, they refuse to engage. This also ties in with the typical way of thinking, that unless you follow this mainstream path, you will not get into college, will not land a good-paying job, and will not be successful.

The bottom line here is the "system" belief that intelligence and grades go hand in hand, with the level of intelligence being reflected in the grades. As soon as intelligence and grades get out of sync, we tend ask *what's wrong?* Why? Because it goes against the belief that the two parallel each other. But in fact, there is nothing wrong at all. Deep down, Indigos know that this is an old paradigm, and they don't choose to conform to it. In short, they know inwardly that intelligence and grades don't necessarily fit together.

So why is she doing this? Well, as an Indigo, your daughter on a deeper level is understanding the superficial nature of it all. She may strongly feel that there is no purpose to studying material that holds no interest for her and does not resonate with her. She may be angry that she had no say in choosing courses that would appeal to her. The present system is designed not to allow choice, except for elective courses. As I mentioned earlier, because Indigos are nonconformists, they will not engage in anything that is superficial, one-dimensional, or seemingly linear in nature. And jumping through the hoops of the educational system, to most of them, is construed as one-dimensional. They recognize the game, and they don't like playing it.

So what to do? One way to get through all of this is to allow her to find the creative aspect in the study. Short of quitting school or finding alternative instruction methods, it is important to understand that for her as an Indigo to help change the system (which is part of her global missions), she has to be in the heart of the system she is helping to change. In order for her to get through it all, it is necessary to discover creative ways and use creative tools. Sometimes, the method of learning can change through the use of various creative means such as color, music, or art for example.

Everybody learns differently, and your daughter needs to discover her method of receiving and understanding information. Sometimes, drawing a picture rather than writing down words on a line may help in the understanding. I have talked to many people who have used song or dance to help them memorize information. Others may use color to highlight or underline important points. Your daughter may have strengths in the visual, auditory, or sensory aspects. She may absorb information more visually than auditory. The use of analogies or scenarios that they can relate to can help Indigos understand concepts or ideas. It can change their whole perspective and understanding of the material.

I hope this whole mouthful of information can assist you with your daughter. I wish you all the best, especially as an Indigo parent.

From an Indigo teen:

Q: As a young child, I would see energies around people. I could see their auras and colored lights around them. I can also see energy in the air and feel it running through my hands. I've noticed that when people talk about spiritual things or get very emotional, then I see their energy much more clearly. I also see spirits, but sometimes it scares me because I don't know what I'm supposed to do with what I see. Usually these spirits are shadows and figures, and they don't scare me, but sometimes they visit me in my dreams. What do I do about this? Am I crazy?

A: We all have a natural psychic ability. It is not something special or exclusive to a chosen few. I believe that our natural state is truly intuitive. It is who we are. But one of the differences that I have noticed with Indigos (as well as with the next generation—the Crystal children) is that they are open energetically. In other words, your ability is real and you are consciously aware of it. This is one of the hallmarks of being a Super Sensitive child. You are *conscious* of your energy, but how to channel it or do something purposeful with it can be a challenge.

It took me a long time to determine for what purpose I was going to use my psychic abilities. I had many fears to process: fear of what others might think of me; fear of being wrong; fear of being ridiculed or put down. I had to flush out all the ego issues that stood in the way of accepting myself for who I was and embracing my inherent state. You can't run away from who you are, because it will always keep showing itself anyway.

You are not crazy. Crazy is the self-talk, the ego that creeps in trying to discount our true self. What you are meant to do with this will unfold in its own time. For now, honor yourself. Accept that what you see, feel, hear, or sense is very real. You have a strong connection with angels. While we are awake, our mind often jumps in and tries to censor what we are intuiting. The dream time is often when we have visits from loved ones who have passed over, or messages from angels and spirit guides, because it is during this time that the mind has temporarily moved aside to allow your spirit to come forward.

So allow yourself just to be with it. Do not get caught up in the whats or the hows. And trust—that's key to your acceptance and confidence in who you are.

From a parent seeking Indigo support groups:

Q: Can you tell me if there are any camps or groups that cater to Indigos/Crystals and families where we can go and hang out with others of like mind?

A: Thanks for your question. Right now, there are a number of camps springing up all over North America that cater to what I call the Super Sensitives: Indigos, Crystals, parents, families, and friends. A good place to start looking would be resources at http://www.campindigo.org.

These groups have been formed by people like you who have felt the need to connect with others of like mind and energy. I have met a number of people who have started businesses or groups that are geared to activities that cater to Indigos and Crystals; two examples are YogaKids in California and ReikiKids on Vancouver Island, British Columbia.

AFTERWORD

I have had many e-mails asking whether there are different types of Indigos. I have also come across written material that categorizes Indigos based on a range of decades of birth. The decade from 1968 to 1978 has been designated Alpha Indigo or First Wave by those who need to affix labels to things. Subsequent decades have received other labels, and each described with slightly different characteristics, personalities, attitudes, and purposes.

It is normal in this human world to want to fit in, to belong, to be part of a group and know we are not alone. The fuller and more specific the description of a profile, the more we seem to place our understanding and ultimately our security in who we are.

But Indigos do not need someone else telling them who they are. The security of being Indigo lies in shining our light and authentically showing ourselves, not focusing our energy on which decade we were born in or which specific Indigo label we fall under. While the temporary labels and descriptive boxes are fun and entertaining, they do not have lasting value. I believe that placing energy on delineating subgroups veers away from the main purpose—and that is, to simply *be* Indigos and fulfill our purposes.

So, to you Indigo, go forward with confidence in this life that you chose to be a part of. As Ghandi said, *"Be the change you want to see in the world."*[22]

In my opinion, that is all that is necessary to ultimately survive.

SUMMARY OF KEYS AND TIPS

<u>Keys to Indigo Survival:</u>

Key #1: Know That You Are Here by Choice

Key #2: Determine Your Values

Key #3: Determine Your Personal Operating System

Key #4: Connect with Others of Like Mind

Key #5: Use the Gifts with Which You Were Born

Key #6: Take Stock of Your Strengths and Interests

Key #7: Fall in Love with What Is in Your Heart

Key #8: Resistance to Your Purpose Is Like a Boomerang—It Always Comes Back

Key #9: Experiencing the Dark Night of the Soul

Key #10: Ditch the Sword: Become the Spiritual Warrior

Key #11: Let Go of the Past and Feel the Feelings Fully

Key #12: Escape Mechanisms are not Coping Mechanisms

Key #13: You Feel Different Because You Are!

Key #14: Become Intimate with Your Energy

Key #15: Ground Yourself

Key #16: Set Boundaries and Practice Detachment—Energetic Self-Defense

Key #17: Create Your Personal Filtering System

Key #18: Intuition Is the Language of Spirit

Key #19: Drop the Critical Self-Talk

Key #20: Clear Your Mind to Hear Your Spirit

Key #21: Tune In to Your Spirit through Meditation

Key #22: Trust Your Inner Knowing

Key #23: Bodily Movement Is the Key to Mental Focus

Key #24: It Is Essential to Heal on All Levels

Key #25: Don't Take Yourself Too Seriously

Tips for Indigo Guidance:

Tip #1: Show them honor and respect.

Tip #2: Structure is important but so is freedom to choose.

Tip #3: Communicate clearly and behave honestly, fairly, and with integrity.

Tip #4: Acknowledge and support their intuitive abilities and higher knowledge.

Tip #5: Be aware of and tolerant of their physical sensitivities.

Tip #6: Recognize that Indigos' opinions are worthy.

Tip #7: Help them to cultivate their purpose for being here.

RESOURCES

Educational and Personal Development Businesses/Software

- **Inspiration Software, Inc.**, mind-mapping software for parents, children, and educators that assists in visualizing, learning, organizing, and thinking creatively.
  Web site: www.inspiration.com (USA)
  www.strategictransitions.com (Canada)

- **TimeLessNow.com, Inc.**, offers stress-relief software solutions for wellness. Programs for ADD, test anxiety, better grades, and trauma. Naturally lowers blood pressure, reduces pain, and promotes faster healing of the mind, body, and spirit.
  Web site: www.timelessnow.com

- **The Wild Divine Project** produced a computer program, *The Journey to Wild Divine*, that links biofeedback hardware to your computer to create a wellness experience. It helps players relax and relieve stress through fun breathing and meditation exercises. It is supported by Deepak Chopra, MD
  Web site: www.wilddivine.com

- **MindWorks for Children** was founded by Dr. Roxanne Daleo, a health educator and pioneer in behavioral medicine. She has designed drug-alternative treatments to help children deal with stress disorders. Her audio-visual programs combine stress management, cognitive/behavioral therapy, and biofeedback.
  Web site: www.mindworksforchildren.com

- **Peak Potentials Training** offers personal development training, seminars, and coaching to help people live in their higher selves.
  Web site: www.peakpotentials.com

Focus and Concentration, ADD, ADHD, ODD

- **Fidget to Focus**, books and strategies on innovative ways to deal with ADD, ADHD, and diagnoses.
  Web site: www.fidgettofocus.com
- **Attention Deficit Disorder Association** provides information, resources, and networking opportunities to help adults with ADD and ADHD. It offers numerous audio and video tapes.
  Web site: www.add.org

Mind-Body Healing

- *Neuromuscular Integrative Action (NIA)* uses expressive movement to achieve physical, mental, emotional, and spiritual fitness and well-being.
  Web site: www.nia-nia.com

- **Emotional Freedom Techniques (EFT)** provide relief from pain, diseases, and emotional issues by stimulating energy meridian points on your body by tapping on them with your fingertips.
  Web site: www.emofree.com

- *Reiki* is a Japanese holistic, light-touch, energy-based practice. It reestablishes a normal energy flow of life force energy throughout the body, which can help the body's innate healing ability. It uses a series of hand positions on or just above your body to strengthen the flow of energy through your body.
  Web sites: www.reiki.ca (Canadian Reiki Association)
  www.iarp.org (International Association of Reiki Professionals)

- *Healing Touch* is a holistic, energy-based therapy that for good health and healing. It uses gentle, non-invasive touch to support the human energy system.

Web sites: www.healingtouch.net (USA)
www.healingtouchcanada.net (Canada)

- *Neuro Linguistic Programming (NLP)* is a behavioral technology that uses a set of guiding principles, attitudes, and techniques about real-life behavior.
Web sites: www.nlp.com (USA)
www.nlpcanada.com (Canada)

- *Yoga* is one of the oldest known health practices and is based on the principal that the mind and the body work together. Practicing yoga brings the body, mind, and spirit into balance through poses, stretches, meditations, and breath work.
Web sites: www.yogamovement.com
www.specialyoga.com
www.yogakids.com

- *Tai Chi and Qigong* are ancient Chinese exercises that connect with qi, the life-force energy. They help stimulate and balance the flow through energy pathways of the body. Both exercises combine body movements with meditation, visualization, and breath coordination to promote relaxation and natural balance.
Web sites: www.thetaichisite.com
www.qi.org
www.qigong.com

Music and Inspiration

- **David De Michele**, Crestone, Colorado
CDs: *Through Indigo Eyes*
Passage Through the Central Sun
Web site: www.indigoworldproductions.com
E-mail: info@indigoworldproductions.com

- **Soundings of the Planet**, Bellingham, Washington
CDs: *Ocean Dreams*
What Child Is This
Web site: www.PeaceThroughMusic.com

- **The Mozart Effect Resource Center**, Boulder, Colorado
Web sites: www.mozarteffect.com

- **Baby Einstein Music and Developmental Products**
Web site: www.babyeinstein.com

Schools and Organizations for Indigos and Crystal Children

- **School Indigo**, Idaho
Web site: www.campindigo.org

- **Sudbury Valley Schools**
Web site: www.sudval.org (USA)
www.sudbury.de (Germany)
www.indigosudburycampus.com (Canada)

- **Alternative Education Resource Organization**
Web site: www.educationrevolution.org

- **Montessori and Waldorf Schools**
Web sites: www.montessori.org
www.montessori.edu
www.awsna.org

- **Homeschooling**
Web sites: www.flora.org/homeschool-ca (Canada)
www.homeschoolzone.com (USA)

ENDNOTES

Chapter One: The Indigo Has Landed
1. Ehrmann, Max. *The Desiderata of Happiness: A Collection of Philosophical Poems. 1927*

Chapter Two: Early Shapings
2. Rumi, Jellaludin. Source: http://www.artquotes.net

Chapter Three: Altered Realities
3. Bakr, Abu. *The Oxford Dictionary of Quotations, 3rd Ed.*

Chapter Four: I See Angels, God, and Dead People
4. Schweitzer, Albert. Source: http://www.worldofquotes.com.

Chapter Five: I Just Want to Be Normal
5. Seuss Geisel, Theodor. Source: *ThinkExist.com Quotations.* "Dr. Seuss quotes." *ThinkExist.com Quotations Online* 1 Jun 2006. 19 Jul 2006 http://einstein/quotes/dr._seuss/

Chapter Six: I'm Here to Do—What?
6. O'Neill, Edmund. Source: http://www.inspirationpeak.com

Chapter Seven: Indigo, Crystals, and Cusps…Oh My!
7. Montessori, Maria. Source: http://www.great-quotes.com/children_quotes.htm

Chapter Eight: The Indigo/Crystal Questionnaires
8. Tutu, Archbishop Desmond. Source: http://www.people4peace.net/quotes/

Chapter Nine: The External Hallmarks: Through the Eyes of the Super Sensitive
9. Source: http://en.thinkexist.com/quotation

10. Thoreau, Henry David. Source: http://www.brainyquote.com

Chapter Ten: Know Thyself
11. Source: http://www.disciplelight.com

Chapter Eleven: You Have a Purpose
12. Cayce, Edgar. Source: http://www.all-ez.com

13.Gibran, Kahlil. Source: *ThinkExist.com Quotations*. "Kahlil Gibran quotes." *ThinkExist.com Quotations Online* 1 Jun 2006. 19 Jul 2006 http://einstein/quotes/kahlil_gibran/

Chapter Twelve: Mastering the Emotional Roller Coaster
14. Rumi. The GuestHouse Source: http://www.elise.com/quotes

15. de Chardin, Pierre. Source: http://www.brainyquote.com

Chapter Thirteen: Energy Management
16. Buddha. Source: *ThinkExist.com Quotations*. "Meditation quotes." *ThinkExist.com Quotations Online* 1 Jun 2006. 19 Jul 2006 http://einstein/quotations/meditation/

Chapter Fourteen: Healing and Honoring Your Spirit
17. Gill, Olena. *The Enlightenment Box.* Canada: 2007.

Chapter Fifteen: Understanding the Indigo Mind-Body Connection
18. Wild, Ron. Source: *ThinkExist.com Quotations*. "Ron Wild quotes." *ThinkExist. com Quotations Online* 1 Jun 2006. 19 Jul 2006 http://einstein/quotes/ron_wild/

Chapter Sixteen: Seven Tips for Indigo Guidance
19. Humphrey, Hubert. Source: *ThinkExist.com Quotations*. "Hubert Humphrey quotes." *ThinkExist.com Quotations Online* 1 Jun 2006. 19 Jul 2006 http://einstein/quotes/hubert_humphrey/

20. *The Bible*, New Revised Standard Version Bible, Matthew 5:9. Copyright 1989, by the Division of Christian Education of the National Council of the Churches of Christ in the United States of America. Nashville, TN: Thomas Nelson Inc..

Chapter Seventeen: Readers' Questions Answered
21. Plomp, John J. Source: *ThinkExist.com Quotations.* "John J. Plomp quotes." *ThinkExist.com Quotations Online* 1 Jun 2006. 19 Jul 2006 <ins>http://einstein/quotes/ john_j._plomp/</ins>

Afterword
22. Ghandi, Mahatma. Source: *ThinkExist.com Quotations.* "Mahatma Gandhi quotes." *ThinkExist.com Quotations Online* 1 Jun 2006. 19 Jul 2006 <ins>http://einstein/ quotes/mahatma_gandhi/</ins>

ABOUT THE AUTHOR

Olena Gill, is an author, life coach, professional intuitive, and metaphysician who holds degrees in music, psychology, and metaphysics. She is doctoral candidate in Holistic Life Counseling.

As the owner and facilitator of an integrative holistic health clinic and coaching practice for more than twelve years, Olena has worked with people all over the globe—individually and in groups—to assist them in discovering themselves and finding their inner purpose.

An Indigo survivor, one of her missions in life is to work with Indigo and Crystal children—to help them wake up to their true selves and assist them in navigating through this world.

Since 1994, Olena has conducted workshops on personal and intuitive development, spiritual growth, and mind-body healing and has appeared on numerous television and radio programs. For more information on Olena, her workshops, and her books, please visit her Web site at http://www.indigocrystalcoach.com.

Olena lives and works on beautiful Vancouver Island, British Columbia, Canada.

TO CONTACT THE AUTHOR

If you are interested in:

- Learning more about Olena Gill and her work;
- Being placed on her monthly mailing list;
- Receiving monthly mind-body-spirit newsletters;
- Inquiring about private consultations;
- Receiving information on future books, publications, and products;
- Inquiring about courses, upcoming workshops, or teleseminars;
- Booking Olena for media spots: television, radio, and keynote speaking;
- Connecting with the IndigoCrystalKids Yahoo Groups discussion forum;
- Joining the Indigo-Crystal public Network.

Please visit her Web site at http://www.indigocrystalcoach.com

978-0-595-40203-8
0-595-40203-8

CPSIA information can be obtained at www.ICGtesting.com
Printed in the USA
LVOW131209060313

322993LV00001B/37/A

9 780595 402038